HENRY O. DORMANN
is the president and editor-in-chief of
Leaders Magazine, a quarterly circulated to the world's most distinguished
and influential people. He has spent the
better part of his lifetime collecting the
wit and wisdom of statesmen, writers,
entertainers, scientists, historians, and
other fascinating people.

THE SPEAKER'S BOOK OF QUOTATIONS

HENRY O. DORMANN

FAWCETT COLUMBINE • NEW YORK

A Fawcett Columbine Book
Published by Ballantine Books
Copyright © 1987 by Henry O. Dormann

Library of Congress Catalog Card Number: 86-91061

ISBN: 0-449-90221-8

Cover design by Richard Aquan
Book design by Alex Jay/Studio J
Manufactured in the United States of America
First Edition: April 1987
10 9 8

Grateful acknowledgment is made to the following for permission to reprint previously published material:

C.R. Gibson Co.: quotations from *Apples of Gold* by Jo Petty. Copyright © 1962 by Jo Petty. Reprinted by permission of the C.R. Gibson Co.

Henry Holt & Co.: excerpt from the poem "The Black Cottage" from *The Poetry of Robert Frost*, edited by Edward Connery Lathem. Copyright 1930, 1939, © 1969 by Holt, Rinehart & Winston, Inc. Copyright © 1958 by Robert Frost. Copyright © 1967 by Lesley Frost Ballantine. Reprinted by permission of Henry Holt and Company, Inc.

CONTENTS

INTRODUCTION

Words are frequently condemned: We blame them for not being deeds. But words are the clothing of deeds. They can also be, at their best, the bricks and mortar that build the hopes and bring to life the dreams of man. Such was their power in the Ten Commandments, the Magna Carta, and the Declaration of Independence.

I believe that words *do* count for a great deal. I love words used well. I love to play with them as if they were toys—toys of the mind. I like to savor the eloquent words of others, from Cicero to Reagan. I have long been a collector of the beautiful things produced by the skills of man, and words used well are among the greatest of these creations. My favorite words are those that, without fear, rip to pieces false gods or the undeserved importance of things or people, with a gentle and yet sharp bit of humor.

I cherish the words that help us enjoy the society of which we are a part, enrich our lives, and help us point with anger, chagrin, courage, and especially with humor at those things that challenge our hopes and our goals. Words can be weapons in the battle for the good things. They are also treasures to be preserved, studied, admired, and used with pleasure again and again. Words are gifts given freely—from the lips, from the pen. Usually the creator of the words enjoys the giving and the sharing of the ideas and thoughts they impart, not the exposure that comes from clever creation. You cannot put a price on words; once said, once written, they are shared and enjoyed by all who hear them.

Forgive me if every quotation is not completely accurate or if I have not always given an author's name. Some of these words came to me from the lips of those whose company I have enjoyed during my world travels—from presidents, generals, cabinet members, princes and kings, prime ministers, scholars and students, people in the marketplace and in the hotels, chauffers and taxi drivers, and from the walls of monuments and churches, public buildings—wherever words are used to make a point and from whomever uses them. The collection is scattered. Some selections remain and even cling in my mind; others are on scraps of paper in my desk or in a file; still others in letters I've received. Many have appeared in articles in *Leaders* magazine. There are words here of my own composition as well, and those of my wife, Alice, hidden among the illustrious words of others. My joy is not in authorship or compilation, but in sharing.

Clifton Fadiman tells a story illustrating the kind of "research" that helped me bring this book into being:

> "Nicholas Murray Butler and Professor Bander Matthews of Columbia University were having a conversation and Professor Matthews was giving his ideas as to plagiarism, from an article of his own on the subject. 'In the case of the first man to use an anecdote,' he said, 'there is originality; in the case of the second, there is plagiarism; with the third, it is a lack of originality; and with the fourth, it is drawing from a common stock.' 'Yes,' broke in President Butler, 'and in the case of the fifth, it is research.' "

> —B.A. Bodkin
> *A Treasury of American Anecdotes*

We've discovered that quotations appearing in formal collections may be quoted in one book as having been said by Lincoln, and in another by Mark Twain.

All of which goes to prove our point—that the giver of the words had only the message in mind, and may, even unknowingly, have used words spoken or written centuries ago.

This book is a small sampling from the very personal collection of my favorite playthings of the tongue and of the mind. These are words I've cherished since I found them and have used from time to time, in letters, in speeches, and in conversations. They've served me well as many of them have probably served others before me. And, delightfully, they never seem to wear out. In their repetition they become more familiar and more enjoyable, and certainly more meaningful. What greater luxury can there be than these satisfying words which can never be worn out and can only get richer with continued use?

THE
SPEAKER'S
BOOK OF
QUOTATIONS

1

AGE

Age is the stuff we desperately want when we are very young and don't want at all when we get older. But, like it or not, aging is the one experience we all must share.

Growing old is no more than a bad habit which a busy man has no time to form.

André Maurois (1885–1967)
French biographer and novelist

To me, old age is always fifteen years older than I am.

Bernard Baruch (1870–1965)
American Statesman and Financier
Speech, November 1960, Overseas
Press Club, New York City

Age does not matter if the matter does not age.

Carlos Pena Romulo (1901–1985)
Philippine diplomat, educator, and
former president
Speech upon retirement from the U.N.

When Somerset Maugham was recuperating from the flu an admirer called and asked, "Could I send you fruit, or would you prefer flowers?" He was eighty-eight years old. He told her, "It's too late for fruit, too early for flowers."

> W. Somerset Maugham (1874–1965)
> British author

When I made my debut as a twelve-year-old in Berlin, people used to say, "Isn't he wonderful for his age?" Now they're beginning to say the same thing again.

> Mischa Elman (1891–1967)
> American violinist, born in Russia
> On his 70th birthday

Chauncey Depew met Mary Garden, the Metropolitan Opera star who had a figure equal to her talent. Seeing her in a gown of pronounced *décolletage*, he asked her what keeps her dress up. She replied, "Two things: your age and my discretion."

> Chauncey M. Depew (1834–1928)
> American Lawyer, legislator, orator

I always wake up in the morning a young man.

> Carlos Pena Romulo (1901–1985)

I do not feel any age yet. There is no age to the spirit.

———

Children are a great help. They are a comfort in your old age. And they help you reach it faster, too.

———

How old would you be if you didn't know how old you were?

Ruth Gordon (1896–1984)
American actress, playwright

Nothing is free. Even age. Age is the fee God charges for life.

———————

You can take no credit for beauty at sixteen. But if you are beautiful at sixty, it will be your soul's own doing.

Marie Stopes (1880–1958)
British advocate of birth control

You know you're getting older when the candles cost more than the cake.

Bob Hope (b. 1903)
American comedian

One of the many things nobody ever tells you about middle age is that it's such a nice change from being young.

Dorothy Canfield Fisher (1879–1958)
American author

Youth is the gift of nature, but age is a work of art.

Garson Kanin (b. 1912)
American author

How can I die? I'm booked.

George Burns (b. 1896)
American comedian

I wake up every morning at nine and grab for the morning paper. Then I look at the obituary page. If my name is not on it, I get up.

Harry Hershfield (1885–1974)
American comedian

Old age is like climbing a mountain. You climb from ledge to ledge. The higher you get, the more tired and breathless you become, but your views become more extensive.

Ingmar Bergman (b. 1918)
Swedish movie director and writer

I look so young, I think I'm getting acne.

Alice K. Dormann

We do not stop playing because we are old. We grow old because we stop playing.

One positive advantage to age for me is that I have more time to smell the roses.

Helen Hayes (b. 1900)
American actress

With each year I live, the notion of becoming elderly recedes further into the future.

A ninety-two-year-old man visited his doctor and complained about a pain in his right knee.

"With your age," said the doctor, "what do you expect?"

"I don't know," said the gentleman. "I have here a right knee that has served me well for ninety-two years and it is in pain. I also have a left knee that served me just as long. So, tell me, doctor, what should I expect?"

Michael R. McGarvey, M.D. (b. 1941)
Vice-president, Empire Blue Shield
and Blue Cross
Speech in honor of senior citizens of
Nassau County, N.Y., May 7, 1986

An elderly lady told me, "When I was younger I never went anywhere without a thermometer, a hot water bottle, a raincoat, and a parachute. Now that I'm older I wish I had walked more in my bare feet, had gone more places, and spent more time picking daisies."

Roberta Figer
Deputy commissioner of Senior Citizen
Affairs, Nassau County, N.Y.
Speech, May 7, 1986

You've reached middle age when all you exercise is caution.

———

There is nothing wrong with the younger generation that twenty years won't cure.

———

[7]

If people start letting me know how old I am, and I listen, I might start playing like an old man. So, I don't listen.

Pete Rose (b. 1941)
Cincinnati Reds
On TV, May 11, 1986

2

AMERICA

America is loved and hated—sometimes by those closest to it. All that is
good and all that is bad is here in some
degree, at some time. Ours is a land of
individual dreams, many of which are
realized, many of which die. A world
without America would be a bland
place, for in this nation all things are
tried, all things are hoped.

The youth of America is their oldest tradition. It has
been going on now for three hundred years.

Oscar Wilde (1854–1900)
Irish author and wit

America is a large friendly dog in a small room. Every
time it wags its tail it knocks over a chair.

Arnold Toynbee (1852–1883)
English historian

On Thanksgiving Day, all over America, families sit
down to dinner at the same moment—halftime.

Anonymous

In America, prejudices can be helpful. Mr. Bing made my career by keeping me out of the Met so long: Nothing infuriates the American public quite as much as the notion of a haughty, foreign-born aristocrat being mean to one of its native-born girls.

Beverly Sills (b. 1929)
American opera singer

It's a dream about America, what it means and what it can become, a place where we look to the stars and explore the heavens, but never turn aside from those in need, in the forgotten corners of our country.

Edward M. Kennedy (b. 1932)
Massachusetts senator

There are those, I know, who will reply that the liberation of humanity, the freedom of man and mind is nothing but a dream. They are right. It is the American dream.

Franklin Delano Roosevelt (1882–1945)
32nd president of the United States

Democracy means not "I am equal to you" but "you are equal to me."

———

My dream is of a place and a time where America will once again be seen as the last best hope of earth.

Abraham Lincoln (1809–1865)
16th president of the United States

"Americans always seem to be looking for change. Car is old after two years, a dress no longer in style, so you pitch them away. Same thing wid house, work, family, and love."

> Clare Mayfield
> Character in American novelist Joseph Olshan's
> *Clara's Heart*

Europeans are in love with the American dream. It's like one hundred years ago, but the cowboys have motorcycles and Cadillacs.

> Philippe Cotten
> Proprietor, Guignol's restaurant in New York City,
> Explaining why Europeans are opening
> restaurants in America in the 1980s.

This flight somehow symbolized America as we are trying to make it, an America with a black, an Asian, a woman, and with white men, perhaps the most fully integrated flight ever made, all joining in a common cause. Still, I believe in America's resilience and that we will use this tragedy to rebuild.

> Eleanor Holmes Norton (b. 1937)
> Professor Georgetown University
> Statement to the press on the loss of the
> Challenger Shuttle, January 28, 1986

Can America overcome the fatal arrogance of power?

> J. William Fulbright (b. 1905)
> Arkansas senator,
> "The Arrogance of Power," 1966

The business of America is business and the chief ideal of the American people is idealism.

> Calvin Coolidge (1872–1933)
> 30th president of the United States
> Speech to editors, 1925

In America today, we are nearer a final triumph over poverty than in any other land.

> Herbert Hoover (1874–1964)
> 31st president of the United States
> Campaign speech, 1928

Americans are so enamored of equality that they would rather be equal in slavery than unequal in freedom.

> Alexis Charles Henri Maurice Clérel de Tocqueville
>   (1805–1859)
> French historian
> *Democracy in America*, 1835

America's great achievement has been business. The business of business is to take part in the creation of the Great Society. The only basic principle of authority in the American nation is God.

> Henry R. Luce (1898–1967)
> Cofounder, publisher of *Time* magazine
> *Time*'s obituary, 1967

America's present need is not heroics but healing; not
nostrums but normalcy; not revolution but restoration; not surgery but serenity; not the dramatic but the
dispassionate; not experiment but *equipoise*; not submergence in internationality but sustainment in triumphant nationality.

> Warren G. Harding (1865–1923)
> 29th president of the United States
> Speech in Boston, 1920

Most Americans live in small towns and think Europe
is fully of dirty despicable foreigners, which is ironic
because America is a land of foreigners.... Americans
go from one dreary Holiday Inn to another and are
searching desperately for their sanitized lavatory
seats and their iced Coca-Cola. Americans are like bad
Bulgarian wine. They don't travel well.

> Bernard Falk
> Host of "Breakaway," BBC program
> Interview by Ted Koppel on a show concerning
>   terrorism and tourism in April, 1986; also reported
>   in May 1, 1986 issue of *Travel Weekly*

Americans usually believe that nothing is impossible.

> Lawrence S. Eagleburger, (b. 1930)
> President, Kissinger Associates, Inc.

The strength of America—the strength of its management, the strength of its simple-minded people! Meaning they know the difference between good and bad. There's only one safe country in the world, and that's the United States.

> Meshulam Riklis (b. 1923)
> Chairman of the Board,
>   Rapid-American Corporation

America is an adorable woman chewing tobacco.

> Auguste Bartholdi (1834–1904)
> French sculptor of Statue of Liberty
> Comment made during fund-raising trip for Statue in 1871;
>   quoted in a letter by Claude Singer, VP, Chemical Bank,
>   in a letter to *The New York Times*, May 3, 1986

3
ART

Art covers all areas of which I am in awe. I've tried to collect the art that I enjoy, understand, and find fulfilling, whether in the form of a painting, a sculpture, a fine piece of tableware, or a chair. When an object is the result of considered thought, brilliant interpretation, and skilled craftsmanship, it is a treasure to own, to study, and to glory in possessing. All art, whether it pleases us or not, helps to add color, excitement, joy, or sadness and, most often, a sense of awe to our life's experience.

Modern art is what happens when painters stop looking at girls and persuade themselves that they have a better idea.

John Ciardi (b. 1916)
American poet
Saturday Review, 1966

I once had the nerve to ask Picasso the question "What is art?"

He answered, "Art is a lie which makes us see the truth."

James Dickey (b. 1923)
American author
Dick Cavett Show

The artist Maxfield Parrish was relaxing in his studio, taking a break from work and having tea with his model. He heard his wife approaching. "Hurry," he said to the model, "my wife will be suspicious if we are not working. Take off your clothes."

Maxfield Parrish (1870–1966)
American artist

I paint things as they are. I don't comment. I record.

Henri de Toulouse-Lautrec (1864–1901)
French painter and lithographer

The true function of art is to edit nature and so to make it coherent and lovely. The artist is a sort of impassioned proofreader, blue-pencilling the bad spelling of God.

H.L. Mencken (1880–1956)
American critic and author

A rich American visited Picasso's studio and paused in front of a painting. "What does this picture represent?" she asked.

"Two hundred thousand dollars," replied Picasso.

Pablo Picasso (1881–1973)
Spanish artist

Appreciation of works of art requires organized effort and systematic study. Art appreciation can no more be absorbed by aimless wandering in galleries than can surgery be learned by casual visits to a hospital.

> Dr. Albert C. Barnes (1798–1870)
> Collector and donor,
> Barnes Museum, Philadelphia

When I judge art, I take my painting and put it next to a God-made object like a tree or flower. If it clashes, it is not art.

> Marc Chagall (1887–1985)
> Russian painter working in France

I see little of more importance to the future of our country and of civilization than full recognition of the place of the artist. If art is to nourish the roots of our culture, society must set the artist free to follow his vision wherever it takes him.

> John F. Kennedy (1917–1963)
> 35th president of the United States
> Speech honoring Robert Frost,
>   Amherst College, October 1963

Let's create enigmas for posterity.

> Francoise Gilot (1921–1986)
> French artist,
> Mistress of Pablo Picasso
> Reminiscences, in an interview, explaining how
>   she and Picasso included her sketches
>   in his sketchbooks as a joke

People who love art really do need it in the same way they need oxygen.

> Martin Zimet (b. 1931)
> President, French & Company
> *Town and Country* magazine, September 1985

All art is quite useless.

> Oscar Wilde (1854–1900)
> Irish author and wit
> *The Picture of Dorian Gray*

In art the best is good enough.

> Johann Wolfgang von Goethe (1749–1832)
> German poet and philosopher
> *Italian Journey*, March 3, 1787

4
BUSINESS

Business is the work of the skilled and the creative; they make things happen. As Henry Luce once pointed out, the "business of business is to take part in the creation of the Great Society." Those who scorn business never say it should not exist—rather that it should not exist for profit, but simply to do more for more people and be better and better at doing it. Being better *is* the eternal pursuit of the businessman. In fact, it might be easy to demonstrate that without the striving of business for an earned profit, there could *be* no "better."

Don't try to buy at the bottom and sell at the top. This can't be done—except by liars.

Bernard M. Baruch (1870–1965)
American statesman and financier

I'm not a driven businessman, but a driven artist. I never think about money. Beautiful things make money.

Geoffrey Beene (b. 1927)
American clothing designer

Paul Galvin at the age of thirty-three had failed twice in business. He attended an auction of his failed storage-battery business and with his last $750 bought back the battery eliminator portion of it. That part became Motorola. When he retired in the 1960s he said, "Do not fear mistakes. You will know failure. Continue to reach out."

Robert Galvin (b. 1922)
CEO and chairman, Motorola Corporation

Education is one of the keys to survival for large corporations in the remaining few years of the twentieth century. We are in transition from an industrial economy to a post-industrial economy where more people are involved in managing information than in producing goods.

Gordon F. MacFarlane (b. 1925)
Chairman and CEO, British Columbia
Telephone Company

I guess I'm considered a hard taskmaster because I expect people to do a day's work for a day's pay. I don't think I'm unreasonable. I used to do a day-and-a-half's work for a half-day's pay. Perhaps I'm a vanishing breed.

Leona Helmsley
President, Helmsley Hotels

The name of the game in the United States is to sue. It's a national pastime. We probably sue more than any other country and thank God we do. It's the little guy who brings the little suit that makes life safer for all of us.

Melvin M. Belli (b. 1907)
American attorney and author

Message to corporate leaders: Bring your corporation out of the organizational swamp in which we live; spell out your twenty-to-twenty-five-year vision; get your organization structures right; and create human and constructive cultures and values for your people—create an environment in which everyone has the opportunity to do work which matches his potential capability and for which an equitable differential reward is provided.

Elliott Jaques (b. 1917)
Director, Institute of Organization & Social Studies,
Brunel University, Uxbridge

He who speaks ill of the mare, will buy her.

Benjamin Franklin (1706–1790)
American statesman and author
Poor Richard's Almanac

The thing that really worries business today is the great number of people still on their payroll who are unemployed.

———

You can close more business in two months by becoming interested in other people than you can in two years by trying to get people interested in you.

> Dale Carnegie (1895–1955)
> American educator
> Quoted in "Sharing Ideas" newsletter
> for speakers

People don't go to business meetings, parties, and conventions to meet delightful charming people. They go to work. To pick up useful gossip and display their devotion to their jobs, to make new contacts and renew old ones, to publicize their latest triumph and to squelch the latest slander ... you have to be a player to get into the game.

> Katha Pollitt (b. 1949)
> American writer

When a child smiles, he gives pleasure ... so relax. When a businessman smiles, he intends to be pleased, so don't relax.

A business was failing and a consultant was asked to make a survey to determine what to do. After the survey, he recommended: "Start advertising, and use three media: radio, direct mail, and courtesy. The first two will cost money. The third is free, but it is the most important."

The big will get bigger; the small will get wiped out.

> Meshulam Riklis (b. 1923)
> Chairman of the board,
> Rapid-American Corporation

We're losing all across the board—steel, textiles, electrical machinery, paper, lumber—you name it. And I really don't seriously think that we're all that stupid. I don't think almost every industry in the U.S. is losing because we don't know how to compete, or worse, because we don't want to compete. When you're losing a war, the first thing you do is try for a truce before you bleed to death. Right now we're playing innocents abroad in a trade world that is definitely not innocent.

Lee A. Iacocca (b. 1924)
Chairman of the board and CEO,
Chrysler Corporation

We cannot play innocents abroad in a world that is not innocent.

Ronald Reagan (b. 1911)
40th president of the United States
State of the Union Address, 1985

Doing well as the result of doing good. That's what capitalism is all about, isn't it?

Adnan M. Khashoggi
Chairman, The Triad Group of Companies

A conservative industrialist was chatting with President Kennedy in 1962, according to a story in the *Boston Globe* in 1965. Kennedy remarked, "If I weren't president, I'd be buying stocks now." The businessman replied, "Yes, and if you weren't president, I'd be buying them, too."

John F. Kennedy (1917–1963)
35th president of the United States

We don't want inflation and we don't want deflation. What we want is flation.

———————

Writers, professors, businessmen, and lovers are often absentminded; only the last two are dreaming of the pleasures of conquest.

———————

Beware of little expenses: A small leak will sink a great ship.

> Benjamin Franklin (1706–1790)
> American statesman and author
> *Poor Richard's Almanac*

Business is never so healthy as when, like a chicken, it must do a certain amount of scratching for what it gets.

> Henry Ford (1863–1947)
> American automobile manufacturer

Businesses are successful because someone makes the sacrifices others are unwilling to.

> Ki-Jung Kim
> Korean businessman

Never say no when a client asks for something—even if it is the moon. You can always try, and anyhow there is plenty of time afterward to explain that it was not possible.

> Cesar Ritz (1850–1918)
> Swiss cowherder who later created fine hotels bearing his name in Paris and London

I believe that businessmen must fulfill a social function. Entrepreneurs must not only look for their own benefit, but also search for the well-being of society.

Leon Febres-Cordero
President of Ecuador
On a visit to the U.S., 1985

The trouble with this business is the dearth of bad pictures.

Samuel Goldwyn (1882–1974)
American movie producer

God can make a dream. A lawyer makes a corporation.

The survival of business is not only a matter of profits but of prophets, of anticipating ethical consequences.

Verne E. Henderson
President, Revehen Consultants

There is one major reason why private companies make investments in the developing world: profit. Governments may make investments for political reasons. Companies do it for profit. So, a reasonable greed level is expected since profit is a primary motive.

Frank G. Zarb (b. 1935)
Senior partner, Lazard Frères & Co.

Working people have a greatness. Given reasonable leadership they are all too willing to follow, do what is asked of them, and give their best to their employers. They are people. They are complex. They are not willing to be treated like indentured servants. Good business leadership can create and generate the work spirit, the wish to cooperate.

> Arthur E. Imperatore
> Chairman of the board,
> APA Transport Corporation

The secret of business is to know something that nobody else knows.

> Aristotle Onassis (1900–1975)
> Greek shipping magnate

If the profession you have chosen has some unexpected inconveniences, console yourself that no profession is without them, and that all of the perplexities of business are softness compared with the vacancy of idleness.

> Samuel Johnson (1709–1784)
> British journalist, lexicographer, and critic

Business is like a wheelbarrow. Nothing ever happens until you start pushing.

If you deal with a fox, think of his tricks.

> Jean de la Fontaine (1621–1695)
> French author and fabulist
> *Fables*

A young man asked Bernard Baruch if there was a sure way to make a million dollars. Baruch told him that there was one. "All you need to do is to purchase a million bags of flour at one dollar and sell them for two dollars each." Apparently the young man took him seriously. He was August Hecker, the founder of a flour mill company that became the largest of its kind.

Bernard Baruch (1870–1965)
American statesman and financier

Winston Churchill, in reply to a post-war speech in the House of Commons, said, "The substance of the eminent Socialist gentlemen's speech is that making a profit is a sin. It is my belief that the real sin is taking a loss."

Winston Churchill (1874–1965)
British statesman and prime minister

Drive thy business; let it not drive thee.

Benjamin Franklin (1706–1790)
Poor Richard's Almanac

A wise man was asked, "What shall I do to receive the most for my money?" The reply given was "a thing that is bought or sold has no value unless it contains that what cannot be bought or sold. Look for the priceless ingredient."

And what is that?

"The priceless ingredient of every product in the marketplace is the honor and the integrity of he who makes it. Consider the name of the maker before you buy it."

To business that we love we rise betime,
And go to 't with delight

> William Shakespeare (1564–1616)
> *Anthony and Cleopatra*, IV, 4, 20

Dottie Walter, publisher of the "Sharing Ideas" news-letter for speakers, once asked her neighbor, Sally Rand, what message she would like to give business-men. Her answer: "Whatever happens, never happens by itself."

A letter was written to certain people with whom the author had done some unsatisfactory business. "Gen-tlemen: You have undertaken to cheat me. I will not sue you, for the law takes too long. I will ruin you."

> Cornelius Vanderbilt (1794–1877)
> American shipping magnate
> Written to Charles Morgan and C.K. Garrison, his associates in the Accessory Transit Company

The difference in companies is people. I would rather have a first-class manager running a second-rate busi-ness than a second-class manager running a first-rate business.

> Jack E. Reichert (b. 1930)
> President and CEO, Brunswick Corporation

5
CHILDREN

In traveling around the world, I discovered that the true face of a nation is its children. Their smiles, their play, their tears, and their sadness speak volumes. They honestly tell of the character of their nation and its people.

For me, the greatest tragedy of life is that childhood is such a short part of our lives.

Blessed are the young, for they shall inherit the national debt.

Herbert Hoover (1874–1964)
31st president of the United States

Youth is such a wonderful thing. What a crime to waste it on children.

George Bernard Shaw (1856–1950)
Irish playwright

An elderly man said, "Thank God for my sons. My first is a doctor, the second a lawyer, the third a chemist, the fourth an artist, and the fifth a writer."

He was asked, "What do you do?"

He replied, "I have a dry goods store. Not a big one, but I manage to support them all."

Gordon Dakins (b. 1920)
Executive director, National Retail
Merchants Association
Speech, national meeting, 1954

First you teach a child to talk; then you have to teach it to be quiet.

———

The more you love your children, the more care you should take to neglect them occasionally. The web of affection can be drawn too tight.

———

Children have never been good at listening to their elders, but they have never failed to imitate them.

James Baldwin (b. 1924)
American author

If children grew up according to early indications, we should have nothing but geniuses.

Johann Wolfgang von Goethe (1749–1832)
German poet and philosopher

Never have children, only grandchildren.

Gore Vidal (b. 1925)
American author

Parents who are afraid to put their foot down usually have children who step on their toes.

Oriental saying

When I was young, my parents told me what to do; now that I am old, my children tell me what to do. I wonder when I will be able to do what I want to do.

The best way to keep children home is to make the home a pleasant atmosphere–and let the air out of the tires.

Dorothy Parker (1893–1967)
American author and wit

If you have never been hated by your child, you have never been a parent.

Bette Davis (b. 1908)
American actress

As a boy handed his father a poor report card, he asked, "Father, what do you think is my trouble—heredity or environment?"

Familiarity breeds contempt—and children.

Mark Twain (1835–1910)
American humorist

One of the mysteries of life is how the boy who wasn't good enough to marry the daughter can be the father of the smartest grandchild in the world.

———————

Adolescence is the age at which children stop asking questions because they know all the answers.

6
EDUCATION

The more people I meet in all levels of society the more I am amazed at the variety of education offered to the world's inhabitants. It is rare that one cannot learn from another or from life's experiences, if the effort is made. Perhaps that is the secret of achieving a peaceful society: searching for each other's unique and special knowledge.

A mother asked Woodrow Wilson, who was at that time the president of Princeton University, what that university would do for her son. Wilson told her: "We guarantee satisfaction, or you get your son back."

Woodrow Wilson (1856–1924)
28th president of the United States

A new graduate rushed out of his college on graduation day and shouted, "Here I am, world. I have my A.B.!"

The world answered: "Sit down, young man, and I'll teach you the rest of the alphabet."

Good teaching is one-fourth preparation and three-fourths theater.

> Gail Godwin (b. 1937)
> American author
> "The Old Woman"

What school, college, or lecture bring to men depends on what men bring to carry it home in.

> Ralph Waldo Emerson (1803–1882)
> American essayist

Books have to be read. It is the only way of discovering what they contain. A few savage tribes eat them, but reading is the only method of assimilation revealed to the West.

> E.M. Forster (1879–1970)
> British author

Aristotle was asked, "What is the difference between an educated and an uneducated man?" He replied, "The same difference as between being alive and being dead."

> Aristotle (384–322 B.C.)
> Greek philosopher

Some men are graduated from college *cum laude*, some are graduated *summa cum laude*, and some are graduated *mirabile dictu*.

> William Howard Taft (1857–1930)
> 27th president of the United States and
> chief justice of the Supreme Court

EDUCATION

If you think education is expensive, try ignorance.

Derek Bok (b. 1930)
President, Harvard University

A college education seldom hurts a man if he's willing to learn a little something after he graduates.

_____

On being congratulated on what he had done for Harvard University as its president, Charles W. Eliot said, "It is true, as you say, that Harvard has become a storehouse of knowledge. But I scarcely deserve credit for that. It is simply that the freshmen bring so much and the seniors take away so little."

Charles W. Eliot (1834–1926)
President, Harvard University, 1869–1909

Experience is a good school. But the fees are high.

Heinrich Heine (1797–1856)
German poet

Education should be as gradual as the moonrise, perceptible not in progress, but in result.

_____

Ignorance is the curse of God,
Knowledge the wing
wherewith we fly to heaven.

William Shakespeare (1564–1616)
Henry VI, I, 2: 3–4

If you plan for a decade, plant trees. If you plan for a century, teach the children.

————————

I deplore the tendency, in some institutions, to go directly toward training for a trade or profession or something and ignoring the liberal arts. I think it is the foundation of education.

Ronald Reagan (b. 1911)
40th president of the United States

Never learn to do anything. If you don't learn, you will always find someone else to do it for you.

Mark Twain (1835–1910)
American humorist

The graduate handed his diploma to his father and said, "I finished law school to please you and Mom. Now I'm going to be a fireman like I've been saying to you since I was six."

Gene Brown (b. 1926)
American educator

Go to school. I tell you to go to school. I'm well known and I made a lot of money and I lost a lot of money. I'd be better off if I had gone to school longer, and so will you.

Joe Louis (b. 1914)
Heavyweight boxing champion, 1937–1949
TV interview

7

FOOD

One of the special joys I have in my treks around the world is the sharing of a repast with those I meet. It is a rare person who does not enjoy the food of his own nation, and he enjoys it more while sharing it with a stranger. This is the act of welcome and courtesy that is told of in the Bible, a practice of almost every nation in the world. It is a joyous pride one has in sharing one's bread with a friend, or a person soon to be a friend.

Offerings of food have been breaking down barriers for centuries.

Estée Lauder
Founder of the cosmetic firm

If a fly gets into the throat of one who is fasting, it is not necessary to pull it out.

Ayatollah Khomeni (b. 1900)
Iranian religious leader
A Clarification of Questions

French cuisine is so delicious that it's a tribute to Gallic willpower that Frenchmen ever leave the dinner table and attend to business.

> Henry O. Dormann
> *A Millionaire's Guide to Europe*

You only have food where you have money. And there is no money in France. The money is here in New York. That is why New York is becoming a world center for food.

> Gerard Paugaud
> Chef, Aurora, New York City

He who does not mind his belly will hardly mind anything else.

> Samuel Johnson (1709–1784)
> British journalist, poet, and critic

There is no sincerer love than the love of food.

> George Bernard Shaw (1856–1950)
> Irish playwright

I'm on a seafood diet. I see food and I eat it.

All human history attests
That happiness for man the hungry sinner
Since Eve ate apples
Much depends on dinner!

> George Gordon, Lord Byron (1788–1824)
> British poet
> *Don Juan*, Dedication, Canto IV, stanza 99

Eat, drink, and be merry, for tomorrow we diet.

I don't even butter my bread; I consider that cooking.
> Merla Zellerbach (b. 1930)
> American author
> Quoting Katherine Cebrian, *San Francisco Chronicle*, December 21, 1982

To eat is human. To digest is divine.
> Mark Twain (1835–1910)
> American humorist

If you complain about farmers, don't talk with your mouth full.
> On a billboard in the Midwest

At a dinner with James Barrie, George Bernard Shaw, a vegetarian, was served his usual plate. Barrie looked at it, shook his head sadly, and said to Shaw, "Tell me, my good friend, have you eaten that, or are you about to?"
> James M. Barrie (1860–1937)
> Scottish novelist and playwright

The most dangerous food is a wedding cake.
> American proverb

I eat merely to put food out of my mind.
> N.F. Simpson (b. 1919)
> British author
> in "The Hole"

No man is lonely while eating spaghetti; it requires so much attention.

Christopher Morley (1890–1957)
American author and editor

A gourmet who thinks of calories is like a tart who looks at her watch.

James Beard (1903–1985)
American cookbook author

I judge a restaurant by the bread and by the coffee.

Burt Lancaster (b. 1913)
American actor

A good restaurant is one with paying customers inside. But a great restaurant—ah, that is different. Why are there some restaurants with mediocre food that are filled all the time? Because there is some magical spark about them, something extra.

André Surmain
Restaurateur

The two biggest sellers in any bookstore are the cook-books and the diet books. The cookbooks tell you how to prepare the food and the diet books tell you how not to eat any of it.

Andy Rooney (b. 1919)
American broadcast journalist
"Sixty Minutes"

There are pits in the Sole Veronique. Don't let them know. They'll charge extra.

Alice K. Dormann

8

FREEDOM

Freedom is a precious possession. It is amazing to me that those who have it are so casual about it. Perhaps to value freedom for what it is you must have been without it at some time, or have clearly seen the lives of those who have not enjoyed it.

The more you see of the world, the more you realize that the richest ingredient of progress, of life itself, is freedom.

Freedom is truly a short blanket that if it covers one part of the body, leaves some other part out in the cold.

Guido Piovene (1907–1974)
Italian journalist

We are so large that we can neither afford to depend on the world, nor can the world afford to keep us dependent. That is the logic of our freedom, our self-reliance.

Rajiv Gandhi (b. 1944)
Prime minister of India

[42]

The soul of a journey is liberty, perfect liberty. We go on a journey to be free of all impediments; to leave ourselves behind, much more than to get rid of others.

William Hazlitt (1778–1830)
British essayist
Table Talk, On Living to One's Self

The most certain test by which we judge whether a country is really free is the amount of security enjoyed by minorities.

John E.E. Dalberg, Lord Acton (1834–1902)
British historian
The History of Freedom and Other Essays, 1907

Freedom is not something that anybody can be given, freedom is something people take.

James Baldwin (b. 1924)
American author
Nobody Knows My Name

To want to be free is to be free.

Ludwig Börne (1786–1837)
German author
Der ewige Jude

Freedom is the one purport, wisely aimed at, or unwisely, of all man's struggles, toiling, and suffering on this earth.

Thomas Carlyle (1795–1881)
Scottish author
The French Revolution (1837)

The Bill of Rights is a born rebel. It reeks with sedition. In every clause it shakes its fist in the face of constituted authority...it is the one guarantee of human freedom to the American people.

Frank I. Cobb (1869–1923)
Editor, *New York World*

America's greatness has been the greatness of a free people who shared certain moral commitments. Freedom without moral commitment is aimless and promptly self-destructive.

John W. Gardner (b. 1912)
Secretary of Health, Education, and Welfare

Freedom is money in the bank; the more you have, the richer you are.

———————

As for me, I am against freedom, I am for the blessed Inquisition. Freedom is shit, and that's why all these countries founder, from an excess of liberty.

Salvador Dali (b. 1904)
Spanish artist
L'Express, 1975

You can only protect your liberties in this world by protecting the other man's freedom. You can only be free if I am free.

Clarence S. Darrow (1857–1938)
American attorney

Freedom is an indivisible word. If we want to enjoy it, and fight for it, we must be prepared to extend it to everyone, whether they are rich or poor, whether they agree with us or not, no matter what their race or the color of their skin.

> Wendell L. Willkie (1892–1944)
> U.S. industrialist, candidate for president

No man is wholly free. He is a slave to wealth, or to fortune, or the laws, or the people restrain him from acting according to his will alone.

> Euripides (485–406 B.C.)
> Greek dramatist
> *Hecuba*

Intellectual freedom is essential to human society. Freedom of thought is the only guarantee against an infection of people by mass myths, which, in the hands of treacherous hypocrites and demagogues, can be transformed into bloody dictatorships.

> Andrei Dmitrievich Sakharov (b. 1921)
> Russian nuclear scientist

There is a road to freedom. Its milestones are Obedience, Endeavor, Honesty, Order, Cleanliness, Sobriety, Truthfulness, Sacrifice, and Love of the Fatherland.

> Adolph Hitler (1889–1945)
> German chancellor
> Seen on walls of concentration camps,
> signed "Hitler"

We look forward to a world founded upon four essential human freedoms. The first is freedom of speech and expression—everywhere in the world. The second is freedom of every person to worship God in his own way—everywhere in the world. The third is freedom from want.... The fourth is freedom from fear....

Franklin Delano Roosevelt (1882–1945)
32nd president of the United States
Message to Congress, 1941

Freedom is getting up happy and looking forward to the day ahead. Freedom is knowing that you can cope with and enjoy this day, and, very likely, tomorrow, and tomorrow.

Those who expect to reap the blessings of freedom must, like men, undergo the fatigue of supporting it.

Thomas Paine (1737–1809)
American patriot

The Negro needs the white man to free him from his fears. The white man needs the Negro to free him from his guilt.

Martin Luther King, Jr. (1929–1968)
American civil rights leader
Quoted in his obituary in the
New York Times, April 7, 1968

There is no denying that the winds of freedom are blowing, east and west. They are brisk and bracing winds, sweeping out the old and, I believe, ushering in a new era of freedom, an era in which democracy is once again recognized as the new idea.

> Ronald Reagan (b. 1911)
> 40th president of the United States
> Asian tour, April 1986

They tried their best to find a place where I was isolated. But all the resources of a superpower cannot isolate a man who hears the voice of freedom, a voice I heard from the very chamber of my soul.

> Anatoly B. Shcharansky (b. 1948)
> Soviet dissident
> Speech, about his imprisonment,
> New York City, May 11, 1986

9
FRIENDSHIP

What counts most, as I look back over
the years, are not my accomplishments
but rather the friends who worked with
me as partners in these accomplishments. The funny thing about it all is
that the quality and quantity of those
accomplishments are fuzzy and unim-
portant in my mind, while the friendships remain crystal clear in my
memory.

It takes an enemy and a friend, working together, to
hurt you to the heart. The one to slander you, and the
other to get the news to you.

Mark Twain (1835–1910)
American humorist

A friend is one who knows all about you and still likes
you.

A foreigner is a friend I haven't met.

The only safe way to destroy an enemy is to make him your friend.

Friends are made by many acts—and lost by only one.

Real friends are those who, when you've made a fool of yourself, don't feel you've done a permanent job.

Friendship is like putting on pantyhose. You have to get one foot in and then the other, and wiggle around and tug until you get it right, and then pretty soon you say I love these pantyhose—they fit!

Susan Saint James (b. 1946)
American actress,
TV Guide, April 26, 1986

Friends may come and go, but enemies accumulate.

Thomas Jones
Wall St. Journal, 1975

It's easy to make a friend. What's hard to make is a stranger.

Between men and women there is no friendship possible. There is passion, enmity, worship, love, but no friendship.

Oscar Wilde (1854–1900)
Irish author and wit
Oscariana, 1911

A friend in power is a friend lost.

> Henry Brooks Adams (1938–1918)
> American historian
> *The Education of Henry Adams*, 1907

If a man does not make new acquaintances as he advances through life he will find himself alone. Man, sir, should keep his acquaintances in constant repair.

> Samuel Johnson (1709–1784)
> British journalist, poet, and critic
> Letter to Lord Chesterfield, 1755

10
HAPPINESS

In my travels, I've seen people whose only possession was happiness. What a possession it is! It is the armor that makes it possible for them to survive. Maybe that is the reason I can not understand when I see people pushing happiness away from themselves and those they love.

Happiness is the clothing of a world at peace.

Success is getting what you want; happiness is wanting what you get.

Happiness is good health and a bad memory.

Ingrid Bergman (1915–1982)
Swedish actress

Just think how happy you'd be if you lost everything you have right now—and then got it back again.

'Twixt the optimist and pessimist
The difference is droll:
The optimist sees the doughnut
But the pessimist sees the whole.

McLandburgh Wilson
Optimist and the Pessimist

Why do birds sing in the morning? It's the triumphant
shout: "We got through another night."

Enid Bagnold (1889–1981)
British author

To be without some of the things you want is an indis-
pensible part of happiness.

———————

Happiness is the perfume you cannot pour on others
without getting a few drops on yourself.

———————

Some cause happiness wherever they go; others
whenever they go.

———————

Happiness is the only thing you can give without
having.

———————

There is no duty we so much underrate, as the duty of
being happy.

Robert Louis Stevenson (1850–1894)
Scottish author
"An Apology for Idlers"

Happiness is not a station you arrive at, but a manner of traveling.

... There is only one way to achieve happiness on this
   terrestrial ball,
and that is to have either a clear conscience or none at
   all.

> Ogden Nash (1902–1971)
> American humorist
> *I'm a Stranger Here Myself*

We have no more right to consume happiness without producing it than to consume wealth without producing it.

> George Bernard Shaw (1856–1950)
> Irish playwright
> *Candida*, Act I

The happiest women, like the happiest nations, have no history.

> George Eliot (Marian Evans Cross) (1819–1880)
> British author
> *The Mill on the Floss*

11
INDUSTRY

The industrial accomplishments of the human race are amazing if one stops to think about it. Perhaps most men would be bored if they could not establish industrial complexes; some say the reason man has achievements is so that he has something to brag about and be proud of when he returns home to his wife and children. In my travels I have come to know the leaders of industry and find many of them the true heroes of our time, bringing to all society the tools for a better and fuller life. And, in the last decade, their achievements have been more amazing than in any other period of human history.

Don't find a fault. Find a remedy.
                    Henry Ford (1863–1947)
                    American automobile manufacturer

I was made to work; if you are equally industrious, you will be equally successful.

> Johann Sebastian Bach (1685–1750)
> German composer

Men have become the tools of their tools.

> Henry David Thoreau (1817–1862)
> American writer and philosopher

If consumers are asked to make greater sacrifices than industry, this country is going to have the greatest shortage of all—consumers.

> Betty Furness (b. 1916)
> Consumer advocate and World War II
> spokesperson

There seems to be no escape from our difficulties until the industrial system breaks down for some reason or other, as it nearly did in Europe during the Second World War, and nature reasserts itself with grass and trees among the ruins.

> Robert Graves (1895–1985)
> British poet and novelist

A perfume manufacturer ran out of superlatives and phrases to describe his product. Finally, he figured out what to do. He used this phrase in his advertising: "As we could not improve our product, we improved the box."

We are now in the midst of an industrial renaissance, dramatic in character, pervasive in scope, threatening in force, and yet replete with opportunities... particularly in the U.S.

Two centuries ago the tradesman made the difference; a hundred years ago it was a mechanic; in the fifties it was the engineer; but today it is the scientist.

Joseph F. Toot, Jr.
President, The Timken Company

The nature of world industry is rapidly changing. In the United States more than two-thirds of all wage earners today are service workers. In Japan, a country heralded in recent years for its "industrial awakening," half the workers are service workers. The same is true of Europe, where employment in service industries outstrips employment in the manufacturing, mining, and agriculture industries.

Robert D. Kirkpatrick
Chairman and CEO, CIGNA Corporation

Industry is fortune's right hand.

John Ray (1627–1705)
British naturalist
English Proverbs

There is no substitute for talent. Industry and all the virtues are of no avail.

Aldous Huxley (1894–1963)
British author
Point Counter Point

Henry Ford impressed a visitor to his factory when he pointed to a finished car and said, "There are exactly four thousand, seven hundred, and nineteen parts in this model."

Later, the visitor asked an engineer in the company if what Mr. Ford said was true. He shrugged and replied, "I really don't know. I can't think of a more useless bit of information!"

Henry Ford (1863–1947)

Is there any man here or any woman—let me say, is there any child here—who does not know that the seed of war is commercial and industrial rivalry?

Woodrow Wilson (1856–1924)
28th president of the United States
address in St. Louis, 1919

The interests of them who own property used in industry is that their capital should be dear and human beings cheap.

Richard H. Tawney (1880–1962)
British educator
Religion and the Rise of Capitalism

12
THE LAW

Most of us are impressed by the law. Some are impressed with its volume—so many words, so many books. Others are impressed with its completeness, the fact that there always seems to be a law to address each situation. But, in recent years, more have been impressed with the lucrative role lawyers have found in putting together the right words on paper to create mergers, to sue for satisfaction, even to address the questions of life and morality. Although few understand it, all agree that the law is an impressive force within society.

The law and the stage—both are a form of exhibitionism.

Orson Welles (1915–1985)
American actor and director

Law is the backbone that keeps man erect.

S.C. Yuter
American scientist

I submit that an individual who breaks a law that conscience tells him is unjust and willingly accepts the penalty by staying in jail to arouse the conscience of the community over its injustice, is in reality expressing the very highest respect for law.

> Martin Luther King, Jr. (1929–1968)
> American civil rights leader
> "Letter from a Birmingham Jail," 1964

Law is a sort of hocus-pocus science.

> Charles Macklin (1697–1797)
> Irish actor and playwright
> *Love à la Mode*, Act II, scene 1

We are in bondage to the law so that we may be free.

> Marcus Tullius Cicero (106–43 B.C.)
> Roman orator and statesman

The two leading recipes for success are building a better mousetrap and finding a bigger loophole.

> Edgar A. Shoaff

I was never ruined but twice—once when I lost a lawsuit, once when I won one.

> Voltaire (1694–1778)
> French philosopher and writer

Laws are like sausages. It is better not to see them being made.

> Otto von Bismark (1815–1898)
> Prussian chancellor

When you go into court you are putting your fate in the hands of twelve people who weren't smart enough to get out of jury duty.

> Norm Crosby
> American comedian

On the death penalty—these death sentences are cruel and unusual in the same way that being struck by lightning is cruel and unusual.

> Potter Stewart (1915–1985)
> Associate justice, U.S. Supreme Court,
> 1958–1981

Lost is our old simplicity of times. The world abounds with laws, and teems with crimes.

———————

No man is above the law and no man below it; nor do we ask any man's permission when we require him to obey it. Obedience to the law is demanded as a right; not asked as a favor.

> Theodore Roosevelt (1858–1919)
> 26th president of the United States
> Annual message, 1903

The law locks up both man and woman
Who steals the goose off the common,
But lets the greater felon loose
Who steals the common from the goose.

> Edward Potts Cheyney

THE LAW

Now these are the Laws of the Jungle,
and many and mighty are they;
But the head and the hoof of the Law
and the haunch and the hump is—Obey!

> Rudyard Kipling (1865–1936)
> British author
> *The Second Jungle Book*, "The Law
> of the Jungle," Stanza 19

The life of the law has not been logic; it has been experience.

> Oliver Wendell Holmes, Jr. (1841–1935)
> Justice of the United States Supreme Court
> *The Common Law*, 1881

Draw up the papers, lawyer,
and make 'em good and stout.
For things at home are crossways,
and Betsey and I are out.

> William McKendree Carleton (1845–1912)
> American poet

Woman: "It seems to me that they are splitting hairs in there."

Man: "Madam, that is what we do here. We split hairs."

> Conversation overheard in the lobby of the
> Supreme Court, Washington, D.C.

In the thirties two of the great jurists were arguing a point of law. Learned Hand, the distinguished New York Appellate judge said, "But we are talking about a court of justice."

"No," replied the other jurist, Justice Oliver Wendell Holmes, Jr., "it is only a court of law."

Oliver Wendell Holmes, Jr. (1841–1935)

Divorce is a game played by lawyers.

Cary Grant (b. 1904)
British born American actor
Washington Post interview, 1983

13
LEADERS

Since being the publisher of *Leaders* magazine for nearly a decade, it has been my great pleasure to spend time with many of the world's most exciting people: its leaders. The more I talk with them, the more I realize how fortunate the world is to have such leaders. They are well informed and dedicated to bringing a better life to the people whose lives they influence. I find that the longer they are in their role, the less they think about themselves. Of course there are those who abuse their position of power and use it as an avenue for personal gain but they are the minority. Thanks to the number of sincere and knowledgeable leaders at all levels in the world today, more people are better off than they ever have been or than their parents ever were.

The best executive is the one who has sense enough to pick good men to do what he wants done, and the self-restraint to keep from meddling with them while they do it.

Theodore Roosevelt (1858–1919)
26th president of the United States

Asked what his secret was for lasting so long and and being so successful as the president of the University of Michigan, Dr. James R. Angell explained: "Grow antennae, not horns."

James R. Angell (1869–1949)
President, University of Michigan

A company bypassed the next man in line to fill an executive position. The man who was passed up went to the president and complained, saying he had fifteen years of experience with the firm.

The president answered him, "Not so. You have had one year of experience fifteen times."

———

You're right. I have slept around to get where I am today. I've slept in planes, on trains, and once was so exhausted after a big sales meeting that I even fell asleep in a taxi.

They conquer who believe they can. He has not learned the first lesson of life who does not every day surmount a fear.

Ralph Waldo Emerson (1803–1882)
American essayist

What we get out of government depends directly on who we got into government—and it is getting harder and harder to attract good people into government.

Calvin Mackenzie
National Academy of Public Administration

The boss drives his men; the leader coaches them.
The boss depends upon authority; the leader on good will.
The boss inspires fear; the leader inspires enthusiasm.
The boss says "I": the leader "we."
The boss fixes the blame for the breakdown; the leader fixes the breakdown.
The boss says "go"; the leader says "let's go!"

H. Gordon Selfridge (1858–1947)
British merchant

Certainly a leader needs a clear vision of the organization and where it is going, but a vision is of little value unless it is shared in a way so as to generate enthusiasm and commitment. Leadership and communication are inseparable. You can't have one without the other.

Claude I. Taylor
Chairman of the board, Air Canada

Avoid putting yourself before others, and you can become a leader among men.

———

Because of not daring to be ahead of the world, one becomes the leader of the world.

———

Ruling a big country is like cooking a small fish.

> Lao-tzu (604–531 B.C.)
> Chinese philosopher, founder of Taoism
> *The Way of Lao-tzu*, translated by Wing-Tsit Chan

The chief executive who knows his strengths and weaknesses as a leader is likely to be far more effective than the one who remains blind to them. He also is on the road to humility—that priceless attitude of openness to life that can help a manager absorb mistakes, failures, or personal shortcomings.

> John Adair (b. 1933)
> Professor, Surrey University

The final test of a leader is that he leaves behind him in other men the conviction and the will to carry on. . . . The genius of a good leader is to leave behind him a situation which common sense, without the grace of genius, can deal with successfully.

> Walter Lippman (1889–1974)
> American writer and editor
> *Roosevelt Has Gone*, April 14, 1945

I enjoy being in the company of the members of the board, especially when I am chairman of the board.

> Tan Haji Mhamed Noah

We are the leaders of the whole stream of life. We lead it in the same sense that small boys lead a circus parade when they march ahead of it. But if they turn down a side street, the parade goes on.

> Oliver Wendell Holmes, Jr. (1841–1935)
> Justice of the U.S. Supreme Court

That men are divided into leaders and the led is but another manifestation of their inborn and irremediable inequality. Men should be at greater pains than heretofore to form a superior class of thinkers, unamenable to intimidation and fervent in the quest of truth, whose function it would be to guide the masses dependent on their lead.

Sigmund Freud (1856–1939)
Austrian founder of psychoanalysis
Letters

A leader is best
when people barely know he exists.
Not so good when people obey and acclaim him.
Worse when they despise him.
But of a good leader
who talks little
when his work is done,
his aim fulfilled,
they will say
"We did it ourselves."

Lao-tzu (604–531 B.C.)

Nearly all men can stand adversity, but if you want to test a man's character, give him power.

Abraham Lincoln (1809–1865)
16th president of the United States

Nevertheless a prince ought to inspire fear in such a way that, if he does not win love, he avoids hatred; because he can endure very well being feared while he is not hated, which will always be as long as he abstains from the property of his citizens and subjects and from their women.

Niccolo Machiavelli (1469–1527)
Italian Renaissance statesman,
author of *The Prince*

A leader is a dealer in hope.

Napoleon Bonaparte (1769–1821)
Emperor of France
Maxims

Too bad all the people who know how to run the country are busy driving taxis and cutting hair.

George Burns (b. 1896)
American comedian

Preparation makes for leadership, and leadership is service to man.

E. Bruce Heilman
University of Virginia
quoting Dr. Douglas Southall Freeman

14
LOVE OF COUNTRY

Most of us enjoy the gentle taps of life that occasionally serve to remind us of our love for our country. I feel such a tap whenever a plane lands at an airport after a flight from another land. Some feel it when they see the nation's flag or hear patriotic songs, or watch a child waving a flag on television or a movie screen. Others experience it when their country is threatened, insulted, defamed, or its citizens harmed while in other lands simply because they are Americans.

We all seem to have a sensitive nerve that, when touched, reminds us that we do indeed love our country.

I have no startling panacea for the spirit or the blue-print for attainment. But being asked for personal philosophy I perforce have to make the reply intensely personal. It is an alien act for me. That being understood, and personal reference condoned, I want to repeat all that I basically know, which turns out to be exactly what almost all of us know: Love God, be loyal to country, be true to self.

Conrad Hilton (1887–1979)
American hotelier

Patriotism is an arbitrary veneration of real estate above principles.

George Jean Nathan (1882–1958)
American drama critic, author, editor

Ask not what your country can do for you, but rather what you can do for your country.

Marcus Tullius Cicero (106–43 B.C.)
Roman orator and statesman
Speech, 63 B.C., and later by
John F. Kennedy (1917–1963)

One day, the South will know that when these disinherited children of God sat down at lunch counters, they were in reality standing up for the best in the American dream and the most sacred values in our Judeo-Christian heritage.

Martin Luther King, Jr. (1929–1968)
American civil rights leader
Speech, Washington, D.C., August 28, 1963

During the Occupation, but before his imprisonment, King Christian X of Denmark noticed a Nazi flag flying over a Danish public building. He called the German commandant and demanded that the flag be immediately removed. The commandant refused.

"Then a soldier will go and take it down," said the king.

"He will be shot," replied the commandant.

"I think not," retorted the king, "for I shall be the soldier."

The flag was removed.

Christian X (1870–1947)
King of Denmark, 1912–1947

A Frenchman, wanting to flatter the patriotic Lord Palmerston, remarked, "If I were not a Frenchman, I would wish to be an Englishman."

Palmerston was not impressed, replying, "If I were not an Englishman, I should wish to be an Englishman."

Henry John Temple Palmerston (1784–1865)
British statesman and prime minister

Arturo Toscanini arrived at a town on July third during a South American tour with the NBC Symphony Orchestra. He told his disgruntled players that he wished them to assemble at the theater the following morning. The travel-weary players were looking for a couple of day's rest, but they obeyed, albeit with ill grace. When they were assembled, Toscanini asked them to rise and led them through "The Star-Spangled Banner." "Today is the Fourth of July," he said when they finished. And he dismissed them.

Arturo Toscanini (1867–1957)
Italian conductor

Our country! In her intercourse with foreign nations, may she always be in the right; but our country, right or wrong!

> Stephen Decatur (1779–1820)
> American patriot
> Toast, Norfolk, VA, April 1816

"My country, right or wrong" is like saying "My mother, drunk or sober."

> G.K. Chesterton (1874–1936)
> British author
> *The Defendant*, 1901

Patriotism is a pernicious, psychopathic form of idiocy.

> George Bernard Shaw (1856–1950)
> Irish playwright
> *L'Esprit Français*, Paris, 1932

I offer neither pay, nor quarters, nor provisions; I offer hunger, thirst, forced marches, battles and death. Let him who loves his country in his heart and not with lips only, follow me.

> Giuseppe Garibaldi (1807–1882)
> Italian patriot
> From *Garibaldi's Defense of the Roman Republic*, by G.M. Trevelyan.

Patriotism is not a short and frenzied outburst of emotion but the tranquil and steady dedication of a lifetime.

> Adlai Stevenson (1900–1965)
> American statesman
> Speech to an American Legion
> convention, August, 1952

The overwhelming importance of the atmosphere means that there are no longer any frontiers to defend against pollution, attack, or propaganda. It means, further, that only by a deep patriotic devotion to one's country can there be hope of the kind of protection of the whole planet, which is necessary for the survival of the peoples of other countries.

> Margaret Mead (1901–1978)
> American anthropologist
> *Culture and Commitment*, 1970

15
MEN

My collection of quotations about wom-
en far surpasses in number those I've
collected over the years on men.
Whether this is a commentary on the
nature of my personal interests, or on
the fact that there is much more to say
about women, I cannot say. Perhaps it is
a universal habit to speak more about
women than about men.

I go for two kinds of men. The kind with muscles, and
the kind without.

Mae West (1892–1980)
American actress

Until Eve arrived, this was a man's world.

Life isn't fair to us men.
When we are born, our mothers get the compliments and the flowers.
When we are married, our brides get the presents and the publicity.
When we die, our widows get the life insurance and winters in Florida.
What do women want to be liberated from?

> (Apparently the man who wrote this was afraid to sign his name)

Only one man in a thousand is boring, and he's interesting because he's a man in a thousand.

> Harold Nicolson (1886—1968)
> British politician

Men are creatures with two legs and eight hands.

> Jayne Mansfield (1933—1967)
> American actress

Judge not a man by his clothes, but by his wife's clothes.

> Thomas R. Dewar (1864—1930)
> British sportsman
> *Looking Back on Life* by George Robey

Every once in a while nature stops experimenting and creates a man.

There are only two kinds of men—the dead and the deadly.

> Helen Rowland (1876–1950)
> American journalist

All men are alike in the light.

A man asked the clerk in the bookstore, "Have you a book entitled *Man, Master of the Home*?"
   She looked at him for a moment and then replied, "Try the fiction department, please."

Husbands should be like Kleenex, soft, strong, and disposable.

> From the movie *Clue*

Don't accept rides from strange men, and remember that all men are strange.

> Robin Morgan (b. 1941)
> American author
> *Sisterhood Is Powerful*

Men define intelligence, men define usefulness, men tell us what is beautiful, men even tell us what is womanly.

> Sally Kempton (b. 1943)
> American journalist

Man is the only animal of which I am thoroughly and cravenly afraid.

George Bernard Shaw (1856—1950)
Irish playwright

It's easy enough to be pleasant
when life flows along like a song.
But the man worthwhile
is the man who can smile
when everything goes wrong.

Ella Wheeler Wilcox (1850—1919)
American journalist and poet
"Worthwhile"

16
MONEY

Money as state coinage is said to have originated in Lydia in the seventh century B.C. This enabled governments to issue coins whose nominal value exceeded their value as metals. Paper, as money, is very modern—only about 300 years old.

There is little doubt that money is perhaps the universally most interesting object to all of us. Money is a horror, but what it can do is fantastic.

Whoever said money can't buy happiness didn't know where to shop.

Money is always there, but the pockets change.

Gertrude Stein (1874–1946)
American author

I have enough money to last me the rest of my life, unless I buy something.

> Jackie Mason (b. 1931)
> American comedian
> *Jackie Mason's America*

Money and time are the heaviest burdens of life, and the unhappiest of all mortals are those who have more of either than they know how to use.

A foundation is a large body of money completely surrounded by people who want some.

> Dwight MacDonald (1906–1982)
> American essayist and critic

I hate money, but it soothes my nerves.

> Joe Louis (b. 1914)
> Heavyweight boxing champion, 1937–1949

The chief value of money lies in the fact that one lives in a world in which it is overestimated.

> H.L. Mencken (1880–1956)
> American critic and author

This is to be said for the money motive: An eye to the salability of work obliges a writer to take some thought for his readers, and may even help him cultivate a clear, vigorous, economical style.

> Robert Graves (1895–1985)
> British poet and novelist

A billion here, a billion there—pretty soon it adds up to real money.

> Everett Dirksen (1896–1969)
> Illinois senator
> On the floor of the Senate

I'll make the money. You guys will have to figure out how to spend it.

> John H. MacArthur
> Trustee of the MacArthur foundation

I don't like money. I don't like aspirin. But, it seems, I always need both, sometimes for the same reason.

———————

Sure we're after filthy lucre, but it is the role of the universities to clean it.

———————

The power of money is demonstrated no more effectively than when it transforms an oldster into an elderly person whose jokes are always funny.

———————

Alexander Woollcott went to visit Moss Hart at his estate in Pennsylvania. Hart had every inch of the grounds completely landscaped. He asked Woolcott what he thought of the place.

His answer: "Well, it only shows what God could do if He had enough money."

> Alexander Woollcott (1887–1943)
> American author and drama critic

Money & Man a mutual friendship show;
Man makes false Money; Money makes Man so.

> Benjamin Franklin (1706–1790)
> American statesman and author
> *Poor Richard's Almanac*

No man's credit is ever as good as his money.

> E.E. "Ed" Howe (1853–1937)
> American editor and novelist

When a fellow says, "It ain't the money, but the principle of the thing," it's the money.

> Elbert Hubbard (1856–1915)
> American writer and publisher

The only thing that continues to give us more for our money is the weighing machine.

> George Clark (1752–1818)
> American revolutionary frontier leader

After Clarence Darrow had solved a client's legal problem, the client asked, "How can I ever show my appreciation?"

The lawyer replied, "My good friend, ever since the Phoenicians invented money, there has been only one answer to that question."

> Clarence S. Darrow (1857–1938)
> American attorney

Money can't buy friends, but you do get a better class of enemy.

> Somers White
> Former Arizona state senator
> Dottie Walters's "Sharing Ideas" newsletter

I'm tired of Love,
I'm still more tired of Rhyme,
But money gives me pleasure
all the time.

> Hilaire Belloc (1870–1953)
> English poet

One of the hardest things to teach our children about money matters is that it does.

In suggesting gifts: Money is appropriate, and one size fits all.

> William Randolph Hearst (1863–1951)
> American newspaper publisher

There are a handful of people money won't spoil—and we count ourselves among them.

> Mignon McLaughlin
> American writer

Money is like a sixth sense without which you cannot make a complete use of the other five.

> W. Somerset Maugham (1874–1965)
> British author

The safe way to double your money is to fold it over once and put it in your pocket.

Frank "Kin" Hubbard (1868–1930)
American caricaturist and humorist,
as Abe Martin

Always live within your income, even if you have to borrow money to do so.

Josh Billings (1818–1885)
American humorist

Generations of Americans have proven they'll spare no expense to get more and pay less.

Kay M. Fishburn (b. 1944)
Citizens for a Debt-Free America

When it is a question of money, everybody is said to be of the same religion.

Voltaire (1694–1778)
French philosopher and writer

We all have the means to become prosperous. We have to find the balance between our wealth and our needs.

Robert Bourassa (b. 1933)
Premier, province of Quebec

Bing Crosby was asked by a TV interviewer why he had such a calm, unruffled demeanor. Reaching into his pocket, Bing pulled out a tremendous wad of bills. "That helps!" he replied.

Bing Crosby (1904–1977)
American singer and actor

A fund raiser tried to persuade Hollywood movie producer Louis B. Mayer to give money to a charity. "You know you can't take it with you."

"If I can't take it with me," said Mayer, "I won't go."

Louis B. Mayer (1885–1957)
American movie producer

George Raft earned and disposed of about ten million dollars in the course of his career. "Part of the loot went for gambling," he explained, "part for horses, and part for women. The rest I spent foolishly."

George Raft (1895–1980)
American actor

One can relish the varied idiocy of human action during a panic to the full, for, while it is a time of great tragedy, nothing is being lost but money.

John Kenneth Galbraith (b. 1908)
Canadian-born American economist
Writing on The Great Crash of 1929, 1955

Politics has got so expensive that it takes lots of money to even get beat with.

Will Rogers (1879–1935)
American humorist
Syndicated column, 1931

Someone who's obsessed with making money to the exclusion of other goals in life has likely forgone the possibility of the acceptance in God's kingdom.

Jimmy Carter (b. 1924)
39th president of the United States

There's no money to be made at the bottom. There's no money to be made in the middle. But there's a lot to be made at the top.

Martin Zimet
President, French & Company

17

MORALITY

Morality is a personal thing. Each of us, through the teachings of our childhood and our experience with others, has developed an unwritten list of criteria of behavior. Too frequently I find that a person's morality is a code by which he believes others should perform toward him, rather than a code guiding his behavior toward others. It is our actual day-to-day behavior that determines and defines our morality.

I'm responsible for what I did, not guilty.

Larry Gitlin

All you can do is try to do the best of your ability, and with all the input and knowledge you get, then hope that the decisions you make are based on what is morally right.

Ronald Reagan
40th president of the United States
Answering questions from a group of
    high school reporters at the White House, 1985.

Morality is a private and costly luxury.

> Henry Brooks Adams (1838–1918)
> American historian
> *The Education of Henry Adams*, 1907

I've looked for answers in many ways—religious, political, humanistic, in different places. I have come to believe there is only one response, the moral response. Whatever we do must be measured in moral terms.

> Elie Wiesel (b. 1928)
> Romanian writer and spokesman
> on the Holocaust

Morality is the theory that every human act must be either right or wrong, and that ninety-nine percent of them are wrong.

> H.L. Mencken (1880–1956)
> American critic and author
> *Chrestomathy*

If the power is for sale, sell your mother to buy it. You can always buy her back again.

> 19th-century Ashani proverb

Morality is the attitude we adopt toward people we personally dislike.

> Oscar Wilde (1854–1900)
> Irish author and wit
> *An Ideal Husband*

The foundation of morality is to have done, once and for all, with lying.

> T.H. Huxley (1825–1895)
> British author
> *Science and Morals*, 1886

Morality is suspecting other people of not being legally married.

> George Bernard Shaw (1856–1950)
> Irish playwright
> *The Devil's Disciple*

What is morality in any given time or place? It is what the majority then and there happen to like, and immorality is what they dislike.

> Alfred North Whitehead (1861–1947)
> British mathematician and philosopher
> *Dialogues of Alfred North Whitehead*

I have to live for others and not for myself; that's middle-class morality.

> George Bernard Shaw (1856–1950)
> *Pygmalion*

I have often thought morality may perhaps consist solely in the courage of making a choice.

> Leon Blum (1872–1950)
> Premier of France during periods
> from 1936–1947
> *On Marriage*

The talent of a meat packer, the morals of a money-changer, and the manners of an undertaker.

William Allen White (1868–1944)
Editor, *Emporia Gazette*
Obituary of Frank A. Munsey, 1925

Time is a great legalizer, even in the field of morals.

H.L. Mencken (1880–1956)
A Book of Prefaces

18
THE PAST

It seems to me that most of us take the past too seriously. When we do, the past becomes a burden on the present and very possibly on our future. My advice is to let it be. The past is past and best forgotten. Or, if not forgotten, just used from time to time as a thing of fun —as a pleasant toy of the mind, to play with when we want reflective amusement or relaxation. In calling upon the past, bring up only the more pleasant things. Bury the unhappy and angry memories. Consider that the past is done and used and cannot be refurbished. Let us live well today and tomorrow without inviting the past to have an influence on either.

If we open a quarrel between the past and the present, we shall find we have lost the future.

Winston Churchill (1874–1965)
British statesman and prime minister
House of Commons speech, 1940

THE PAST

…Here lies my past,
Good-bye I have kissed it;
Thank you, kids,
I wouldn't have missed it.

> Ogden Nash (1902–1971)
> American humorist
> *You Can't Get There from Here*

The past is a work of art, free of irrelevancies and loose ends.

> Max Beerbohm (1872–1956)
> British author and wit

The past is a foreign country; they do things differently there.

> Leslie Poles Hartley (1895–1972)
> English author
> Prologue of *The Go-Between,* 1953

I do not believe in recovery. The past with its pleasures, its rewards, its foolishness, its punishments, is there for each of us forever, and it should be.

> Lillian Hellman (1906–1984)
> American author
> Letter to the Un-American Activities Committee
> of the House of Representatives, May, 1952

Layer upon layer, past times preserve themselves in the city until life itself is finally threatened with suffocation; then, in sheer defense, modern man invents the museum.

> Lewis Mumford (b. 1895)
> American author
> *The Culture of Cities* 1938

Let the past drift away with the water.

Japanese saying

I tell you the past is a bucket of ashes.

Carl Sandburg (1878–1967)
American poet
"Prairie," 1918

Recognizing what we have done in the past is a recognition of ourselves. By conducting a dialogue with our past, we are searching how to go forward.

Kiyoko Takeda
Professor, International Christian
University, Tokyo

The past has little importance to most of us for most things, except for the year of a cognac.

Jean-Marie Beulque (b. 1939)
Public Information Officer Bureau du Cognac
Cognac, France, 1984

Sure we respect the past. We keep it in bottles.

Gerard Stürm (b. 1928)
Director Public Information Bureau du Cognac
Cognac, France, 1984

Here's to the past. Thank God it's past!

———————

…and the historical sense involves a perception, not only of the pastness of the past, but of its presence; the historical sense compels a man to write not merely with his own generation in his bones, but with the feeling that the whole of the literature of Europe from Homer and within it the whole of the literature of his own country has a simultaneous existence and composes a simultaneous order.

> T.S. Eliot (1888–1965)
> American-born English poet
> *Tradition and the Individual Talent*, 1917

History is more or less bunk.

> Henry Ford (1863–1947)
> American automobile manufacturer
> Witness in his libel suit against the
> *Chicago Tribune*, May 1916

19
PEACE

Few would challenge the idea that peace is the most precious and most elusive condition on earth. Aged as the earth may seem to us, it is obvious that it is still uncivilized if its inhabitants cannot live in peace. Children do battle in the home and at school because they are children. Adults do battle whenever they disagree because they, too, are still children.

The work, my friends, is peace. More than an end of this war—and end of the beginning of our wars. I ask you to keep up your faith. The only limit to our realization of tomorrow will be our doubts of today.

Franklin Delano Roosevelt (1882–1945)
32nd president of United States
Fireside chat

The Senate Armed Services Committee asked Dr. Robert Oppenheimer, as a member of the Manhattan Project, if there was any defense against a nuclear weapon. He replied, "Certainly. Peace."

> J. Robert Oppenheimer (1904–1967)
> Director, Institute for Advanced Studies,
> Princeton, NJ

A peace which depends upon fear is nothing but a suppressed war.

> Henry Van Dyke (1852–1933)
> American poet

Peace has its victories, but it takes a brave man to win them.

> Ralph Waldo Emerson (1803–1882)
> American essayist

A government official was discussing Prime Minister Ramsay MacDonald's point of view on peace. "The desire for peace," he said, "does not necessarily ensure peace."

MacDonald replied, "Quite true. Neither does the desire for food satisfy hunger. But at least it gets you started toward a restaurant."

> James Ramsay MacDonald (1866–1937)
> British prime minister, 1924, 1929–1935

The pursuit of peace by the leaders of the USSR and the USA reminds me of the cat and the dog who were so busy watching each other that they never noticed the mice eating their food.

God and politicians willing, the United States can declare peace on the world, and win it.

> Ely Culbertson (1891–1955)
> American bridge player

You have to take chances for peace, just as you take chances in war. The ability to get to the verge without getting into the war is the necessary art. If you try to run away from it, if you are scared to go to the brink, you are lost.

> John Foster Dulles (1888–1959)
> Secretary of state

Peace is more precious than a piece of land.

> Anwar al-Sadat (1918–1981)
> President of Egypt
> Speech, Cairo, 1978

The only thing that I do properly, with all my heart, I do not wish to do again. I have only known how to be a good general, and it is to peace henceforth that I want to dedicate all my time, all my labors.

> Dwight D. Eisenhower (1890–1969)
> 34th president of the United States
> Explaining his decision to run for president

It must be a peace without victory.... Only a peace between equals can last.

> Woodrow Wilson (1856–1924)
> 28th president of the United States
> Address, Senate

To be prepared for war is one of the most effectual means of preserving peace.

> George Washington (1732–1799)
> First president of the United States
> Address to Congress, January 8, 1790

I love war. . . . Peace will be hell for me.

> George S. Patton, Jr. (1885–1945)
> American general
> Letter to his wife

I intend to leave after my death a large fund for the promotion of the peace idea, but I am skeptical as to its results. The savants will write excellent volumes. There will be laureates. But wars will continue just the same until the forces of the circumstances render them impossible.

> Alfred Nobel (1833–1896)
> Swedish munitions manufacturer and
>   father of the Nobel Awards
> Public statement, 1890

War is an invention of the human mind. The human mind can invent peace.

> Norman Cousins (b. 1912)
> Editor, *Saturday Review*
> *Who Speaks for Man*, 1953

True, lasting peace cannot be secured through the strength of arms alone. Among free peoples, the open exchange of ideas ultimately is our greatest security.

> Ronald Reagan (b. 1911)
> 40th president of the United States

20
PEOPLE

The nice thing about people is that there are so many of them, and so many varieties. Anyone can find enough people with whom to be friendly, to work, and to share the riches of life on this wonderful planet.

I drink to make other people interesting.

Sign seen in a bar

What is a cynic? A man who knows the price of everything and the value of nothing.

Oscar Wilde (1854–1900)
Irish author and wit
Lady Windemere's Fan, 1892

People don't change. Only their costumes do.

Gene Moorse
Display arranger, Tiffany

After being asked by the Nazis to establish anti-Jewish legislation, the King of Denmark said, "But you see, there isn't any Jewish problem here. We do not consider ourselves inferior to them."

King Christian X of Denmark (1870–1947)
Imprisoned in 1943 for refusing
anti-Jewish legislation

God bears with imperfect beings, and even when they resist His goodness. We ought to imitate this merciful patience and endurance. It is only imperfection that complains of what is imperfect. The more perfect we are, the more gentle and quiet we become toward the defects of other people.

François de Fenelon (1651–1715)
French author,
Archbishop of Cambray

I was so shy, I was like an ingrown toenail.

Barbara Rush (b. 1929)
American actress

President Reagan was speaking in Seattle of those people who continue to criticize his efforts. He said, "They sort of remind me of the fellow who was asked which was worse, ignorance or apathy, and he said, 'I don't know and I don't care.'"

Ronald Reagan (b. 1911)
40th president of the United States

There are three things extremely hard: steel, a diamond, and to know one's self.

> Benjamin Franklin (1706–1790)
> American statesman and author
> *Poor Richard's Almanac*

I believe every person has a heart, and if you can reach it, you can make a difference.

> Uli Derickson
> Flight attendant on
> hijacked TWA Flight #847, 1985

Some people can stay longer in an hour than others can in a week.

> William Dean Howells (1837–1920)
> American author

If you can't get people to listen to you any other way, tell them it's confidential.

> *Farmer's Digest*

I have great faith in fools; self-confidence, my friends call it.

> Edgar Allan Poe (1809–1849)
> American author

There are people who have money and people who are rich.

> Coco Chanel (1883–1971)
> French couturier

There are people who eat the earth and eat all the people on it, like in the Bible with the locusts. And other people who stand around and watch them eat it.

Lillian Hellman (1906–1984)
American author
The Little Foxes

There are two kinds of people who blow through life like a breeze.
And one kind is gossipers, and the other kind is gossipees...

Ogden Nash (1902–1971)
American humorist
I'm a Stranger Here Myself

In spite of everything, I still believe that people are really good at heart.

Anne Frank (1929–1945)
Dutch-Jewish author
The Diary of a Young Girl,
July 15, 1944

21
POLITICS

Few agree whether politics is a profession or a game. Whatever it may be, politics is a dominating force that so-called civilized men and women use to establish authority and power, supposedly for the good of a nation's people. Whatever its purpose, it is a fascinating preoccupation. For me, it has been a spectator sport, one I alternately enjoy, admire, and despise. The least that can be said about politics is that so many people are preoccupied with it, full or part-time. Perhaps that is why this section of my collection of eloquent words is so large.

Princes and governments are by far more dangerous than other elements within a society.

Niccolo Machiavelli (1469–1527)
Italian Renaissance statesman
and author of *The Prince*, 1513

In war you can be killed only once. In politics, many times.

Winston Churchill (1874–1965)
British statesman and prime minister

Forgive your enemies, but never forget their names.

John F. Kennedy (1917–1963)
35th president of the United States

Political success is the ability, when the inevitable oc-
curs, to get credit for it.

Dr. Laurence J. Peter (b. 1919)
American author and psychologist

Politicians and roosters crow about what they intend
to do. The roosters deliver what is promised.

A conservative is a person who does not think anything should be done for the first time.

Frank Vanderlip (1864–1937)
American financier

It is not a government's obligation to provide services,
but to see that they are provided.

Mario Cuomo (b. 1932)
Governor of New York

In politics as on the sickbed, people toss from one side
to another, thinking they will be more comfortable.

Johann Wolfgang von Goethe (1749–1832)
German poet and philosopher

If it looks like a duck, quacks like a duck, and walks like a duck, it is probably a horse.

> Theodoro F. Valencia (b. 1928)
> American newspaper columnist, on
> Philippine elections

Political history is far too criminal a subject to be a fit thing to teach children.

> W.H. Auden (1907–1973)
> British-born American poet

You punch me, I punch back. I do not believe it is good for one's self-respect to be a punching bag.

> Edward Koch, (b. 1924)
> Mayor of New York City

Man's capacity for justice makes democracy possible, but his inclination to injustice makes democracy necessary.

> Reinhold Niebuhr (1892–1971)
> American pastor and theologian
> *The Children of Light and
> the Children of Darkness*, 1944

Women are being considered as candidates for vice-president of the United States because it is the worst job in America. It's amazing that men will take it. A job with real power is first lady. I'd be willing to run for that. As far as the men who are running for president are concerned, they aren't even people I would date.

> Nora Ephron (b. 1941)
> American author
> Lecture, San Francisco, 1983

Ninety percent of the politicians give the other ten percent a bad reputation.

Henry Kissinger (b. 1923)
American diplomat, secretary of state

A politician thinks of the next election—a statesman, of the next generation.

James Freeman Clarke (1810–1888)
American clergyman

You hear politics until you wish that both parties were smothered in their own gas.

Woodrow Wilson (1856–1924)
28th president of the United States

The marvel of all history is the patience with which men and women submit to burdens unnecessarily laid upon them by their governments.

William E. Borah (1865–1940)
Idaho senator, 1906–1940

I know that when things don't go well, they like to blame the president, and that is one of the things presidents are paid for.

John F. Kennedy (1917–1963)

Get all the fools on your side and you can be elected to anything.

Frank Dane

Reagan won because he ran against Jimmy Carter. Had he run unopposed, he would have lost.

Mort Sahl (b. 1927)
American comedian

When the 1968 Democratic convention was held in Chicago, the then-Mayor Richard Daley said at a press conference, "The police are here not to create disorder. They are here to preserve disorder."

Richard M. Daley (1902–1976)
Mayor of Chicago

This is the first convention of the space age—when a candidate can promise the moon and mean it.

David Brinkley (b. 1920)
American broadcast journalist

In 1958, when he was speaking to members of the Gridiron Club in Washington, and it was known he would seek the Democratic nomination, John F. Kennedy said, "I have just received the following wire from my generous Daddy: 'Dear Jack—Don't buy a single vote more than is necessary. I'll be damned if I am going to pay for a landslide.' "

John F. Kennedy (1917–1963)

"For the first six months, you should listen and not become involved in debate," Disraeli advised a newly elected member of Parliament.

"But," the man replied, "my colleagues will wonder why I do not speak."

"Better they should wonder why you do not speak," explained Disraeli, "than why you do."

> Benjamin Disraeli (1804–1881)
> British prime minister

Democracy substitutes election by the incompetent many for appointment by the corrupt few.

> George Bernard Shaw (1856–1950)
> Irish playwright

Be silent as a politician, for talking may beget suspicion.

> Jonathan Swift (1667–1745)
> Irish satirist

Bad officials are the ones elected by good citizens who do not vote.

> George Jean Nathan (1882–1958)
> American drama critic, author, editor

Democrats can't get elected unless things get worse, and things won't get worse unless they get elected.

> Jeane Kirkpatrick (b. 1926)
> Former American ambassador to the U.N.

I can think of nothing more boring for the American people than to have to sit in their living rooms for a whole half-hour looking at my face on their television screens.

> Dwight D. Eisenhower (1890–1969)
> 34th president of the United States

A diplomat is one who can tell a man he's open-minded when he means he has a hole in his head.

A statesman is a politician who has been dead ten or fifteen years.

> Harry S. Truman (1884–1972)
> 33rd president of the United States
> *New York World Telegram and Sun*,
> April 12, 1958

It has been said that democracy is the worst form of government except all others that have been tried.

> Winston Churchill (1874–1965)

Nothing which is morally wrong can ever be politically right.

There are two ways to empty a room in Washington. Hold a fund raiser for a defeated candidate, or a debate on federalism.

> Charles S. Robb (b. 1939)
> Governor of Virginia

Winston Churchill was asked why he got into politics. He replied, "Ambition, pure unadulterated ambition."

Then asked what made him stay in politics, he replied, "Anger, pure unadulterated anger."

Winston Churchill (1874–1965)

Ambassador Clare Booth Luce commented on Senator Wayne Morse of Oregon switching from Republican to Democrat in 1956: "Remember, whenever a Republican leaves one side of the aisle and goes to the other, it raises the intelligence quotient of both parties."

Clare Booth Luce (b. 1903)
American journalist, playwright, and politician

It is more profitable for your Congressman to support the tobacco industry than your life.

Jackie Mason (b. 1931)
American comedian,
Jackie Mason's America

Senator George H. Moses complained to Calvin Coolidge that a man being considered for a Republican senatorial nomination was an "out-and-out S.O.B."

President Coolidge agreed. "That may be," he said, "but there's a lot of those in the country and I think they are entitled to representation in the Senate."

Calvin Coolidge (1872–1933)
30th president of the United States

An ambassador is an honest man sent abroad to lie for his country.

> Henry Wotton (1568–1639)
> British writer and diplomat
> *Christopher Fleckmore's Album*, 1604

Have you ever seen a candidate talking to a rich person on television?

> Art Buchwald (b. 1925)
> American columnist

A man of few words, Calvin Coolidge explained why: "I found out early in life that you never have to explain something you haven't said."

> Calvin Coolidge (1872–1933)

The man with the best job in the country is the vice-president. All he has to do is get up every morning and say, "How is the president?"

> Will Rogers (1879–1935)
> American humorist

In a debate, General Tucker said of his political opponent, John Allen, that while he had been a general in the Army of the Confederacy, Allen had been only a private.

Allen replied, "I admit I was only a private. In fact, I was a sentry who stood guard over the general when he slept. And now, all you fellows who were generals and had privates stand guard over you, vote for General Tucker. But all you boys who stood guard over a general, vote for Private John Allen."

They did. He became Congressman John Allen.

I would not like to be a political leader in Russia. They never know when they're being taped.

Richard M. Nixon (b. 1913)
37th president of the United States

Few businessmen are capable of being in politics—they don't understand the democratic process—they have neither the tolerance nor the depth it takes—democracy isn't a business.

Malcolm Forbes (b. 1919)
American publisher and financier

What sets American democracy apart is the abiding prejudice against party professionals. Wise candidates advertise themselves as ordinary citizens innocent of the dark arts. In this no one has been more successful than Ronald Reagan, arguably the most artfully camouflaged politician in the business.

Karl E. Meyer (b. 1928)
American journalist

After Winston Churchill left the Conservative bench in the House of Commons, he was asked to escort a young lady to dinner. Being a frank young lady, she remarked as they sat at the table, "There are two things I dislike about you."

"And what are they?"

"Your politics and your mustache."

"My dear, do not disturb yourself. You are not likely to come into contact with either."

Winston Churchill (1874–1965)

While I'd rather be right than president, at any time I'm ready for both.

Norman Thomas (1884–1968)
American socialist

When he left his post as secretary of state, Dean Acheson was asked of his plans. "I will undoubtedly have to seek what is happily known as gainful employment, which I am glad to say does not describe holding public office."

Dean Acheson (1893–1971)
Secretary of state and statesman

At an embassy reception, Ann Landers was approached by a rather pompous senator. "So you're Ann Landers. Say something funny."

Without hesitating, she replied, "Well, you're a politician. Tell me a lie."

Ann Landers (b. 1918)
Advice columnist

22
THE PRESS

Having regarded myself as a member of
this following for a number of years, I
can hardly escape prejudice in my feelings about the press. Without their
efforts, much that happens wouldn't,
even though some of what happens
shouldn't. Yet, given the options, few
would elect to eliminate the press and
its activities.

An editor is a person who knows precisely what he
wants but isn't quite sure.

Walter Davenport (1889–1971)
American author

The man who reads nothing at all is better educated
than the man who reads nothing but newspapers.

Thomas Jefferson (1743–1826)
3rd president of the United States

Dead news, like dead love, has no phoenix in its ashes.

Enid Bagnold (1889–1981)
British author

[113]

There is so much to be said in favor of modern journalism. By giving us the opinions of the uneducated it keeps us in touch with the ignorance of the community.

Oscar Wilde (1854–1900)
Irish author and wit

The newspaper is the natural enemy of the book, as the whore is of the decent woman.

The de Goncourt brothers, Edmond Louis Antoine
(1822–1896) and Charles Huot (1830–1870)
French novelists and collaborators

I always turn to the sports pages first, which records people's accomplishments. The front page has nothing but man's failures.

Earl Warren (1891–1974)
Chief justice, Supreme Court

I keep reading between the lies.

Goodman Ace (b. 1899)
American comedian

To the press alone, checkered as it is with abuses, the world is indebted for all the triumphs which have been gained by reason and humanity over error and oppression.

Thomas Jefferson (1743–1826)

An American reading the Sunday paper in a state of lazy collapse is perhaps the most perfect symbol of the triumph of quantity over quality. While whole forests are ground into pulp to minister to our triviality.

Irving Babbitt (1865–1933)
American essayist

The press is free to do battle against secrecy and deception in government. But the press cannot expect from the Constitution any guarantee it will succeed.

Potter Stewart (1915–1985)
Associate Justice, U.S. Supreme Court,
1958–1981

Journalism consists largely in saying "Lord James is dead" to people who never knew Lord James was alive.

G.K. Chesterton (1874–1936)
British author

An editor put this in his newspaper: "If you find an error, please understand it was put there on purpose. We try to publish something for everyone, and some people are always looking for something to criticize."

William Randolph Hearst offered Arthur Brisbane a six months' paid holiday in appreciation of his good work. It was refused.

"There are two reasons why I will not accept your generous offer. The first is that if I quit writing my column for half a year, it might affect the circulation of your newspapers. The second reason is that it might not!"

> William Randolph Hearst (1863–1951)
> American newspaper publisher

A free press is not a privilege, but an organic necessity in a great society.... A great society is simply a big and complicated urban society.

> Walter Lippmann (1889–1974)
> American writer and editor
> Speech, International Press Institute,
> London, May 27, 1965

To me a writer is one of the most important soldiers in the fight for the survival of the human race. He must stay at his post in the thick of fire to serve the cause of mankind.

> Leon Uris (b. 1924)
> American author

A man's judgment cannot be better than the information on which he has based it. Give him no news, or present him only with distorted and incomplete data, with ignorant, sloppy, or biased reporting, with propaganda and deliberate falsehoods, and you destroy his whole reasoning process and make him somewhat less than a man.

> Arthur Hays Sulzberger (1891–1968)
> Publisher, *The New York Times*
> Speech, New York State Publishers Association,
>   August 30, 1948

The facts fairly and honestly presented; truth will take care of itself.

> William Allen White (1868–1944)
> Editor, *Emporia Gazette*,
> Told to George Seldes, American journalist

Write news as if your very life depended upon it. It does.

> Heywood Broun (1888–1939)
> National columnist,
> Told to Jerome Klein,
>   reporter for his high school newspaper, 1938

To a newspaperman a human being is an item with skin wrapped around it.

> Fred Allen (1894–1956)
> American comedian and radio star

If a woman is sent to the Middle East ... will she be able to cover stories there as well as a man? Yes. They may think she's a whore, but often they will talk to her more openly than to a male reporter.

Linda Ellerbee (b. 1944)
Broadcast journalist and author
And So It Goes

23
QUALITY OF LIFE

What are the patterns that guide us in setting the quality of our lives? Would that we knew when we were young the things we know when we are older. Then we would make that turn, take that path, go full steam ahead, and do everything right. Or would we? It would have been too bad to miss our mistakes that taught us so much about living. Just as we enjoyed the terror of the roller coaster when we were kids, we must enjoy the terror of life's errors and mistakes. The challenges we meet are the shapers of the quality of our lives.

There are two tragedies in life. One is not to get your heart's desire. The other is to get it.

George Bernard Shaw (1856–1950)
Irish playwright
Man and Superman, Act IV

The trouble with the rat race is that even if you win you're still a rat.

Lily Tomlin (b. 1939)
American comedian

In spite of the cost of living, it's still popular.

Kathleen Norris (1880–1966)
American author

When Albert Schweitzer returned from a visit to Europe after a long stay in Africa, he was asked, "Well, what do you think of civilization?"

He replied, "It's a good idea. Somebody ought to start it."

Albert Schweitzer (1876–1965)
French medical missionary, author
Nobel Peace Prize winner

We are all manufacturers: making goods, making trouble, making excuses.

———

I shall pass through this world but once; any good things, therefore, that I can do, or any kindness that I can show to any human being, or dumb animal, let me do it now. Let me not deter it or neglect it, for I shall not pass this way again.

John Galsworthy (1867–1933)
British author, Nobel winner, 1932

A teacher, noticing how courteous and polite one of her pupils was, wished to praise her and teach the class a lesson. She asked, "Who taught you to be so polite?"

The girl laughed and answered, "Really, no one. It just runs in our family."

———

Fear less, hope more,
eat less, chew more,
whine less, breathe more,
talk less, say more,
hate less, love more,
and all good things will be yours.

Swedish proverb

What I find attractive about the city is that everything is king size—the beauty and the ugliness.

Joseph Brodsky (b. 1940)
Russian poet

Men and automobiles are much alike. Some are right at home on an uphill pull; others run smoothly only going downgrade. And when you hear one knocking all the time, it's a sure sign there is something wrong under the hood.

———

If we were all determined to play the first violin we should never have an ensemble. Therefore, respect every musician in his proper place.

Robert Schumann (1810–1856)
German composer

Optimism: a cheerful frame of mind that enables a tea kettle to sing though in hot water up to its nose.

———————

No one can make you feel inferior without your consent.

> Eleanor Roosevelt (1884–1962)
> American author, lecturer

People are constantly clamoring for the joy of life. As for me, I find the joy of life in the hard and cruel battle of life—to learn something is a joy to me.

> August Strindberg (1849–1912)
> Swedish playwright

Man never sees the worst in himself, except when he shaves.

We're all in this alone.

> Lily Tomlin (b. 1939)

If I had my life to live again, I'd make the same mistakes, only sooner.

> Tallulah Bankhead (1903–1968)
> American actress

Men try to run life according to their wishes; life runs itself according to necessity.

> Jean Toomer (1894–1967)
> American poet

The trouble with life in the fast lane is that you get to the other end in an awful hurry.

> John Jensen (b. 1911)
> American educator
> Quoted in Herb Caen's column, *The San Francisco Chronicle*, December 2, 1982

Life is 10 percent what you make it, and 90 percent how you take it.

———————

Living is like licking honey off a thorn.

———————

It's a funny thing about life: If you refuse to accept anything but the best, you very often get it.

> W. Somerset Maugham (1874–1965)
> British author

The greatest use of life is to spend it for something that will outlast it.

> William James (1842–1910)
> American philosopher

It is not true that life is one damn thing after another—it is one damn thing over and over.

> Edna St. Vincent Millay (1892–1950)
> American poet
> *The Letters of Edna St. Vincent Millay*

The longer I live the more beautiful life becomes. If you foolishly ignore beauty, you will soon find yourself without it. Your life will be impoverished. But if you invest in beauty, it will remain with you all the days of your life.

Frank Lloyd Wright (1869–1959)
American architect

A life spent making mistakes is not only more honorable but more useful than a life spent doing nothing.

George Bernard Shaw (1856–1950)

The art of living is more like wrestling than dancing.

Marcus Aurelius Antonius (121–180 A.D.)
Roman emperor

The Triple-A formula for experiencing happiness begins by accepting the moment, appreciating it, and adapting to its opportunities.

———————

Is life worth living? It all depends on the liver.

William James (1842–1910)

All his life he [the American] jumps into a train after it has started and jumps out before it has stopped; and never once gets left behind, or breaks a leg.

George Santayana (1863–1952)
Spanish-born philosopher and poet
Character and Opinion in the United States, 1920

The best part of married life is the fights. The rest is merely so-so.

> Thornton Wilder (1897–1975)
> American novelist and playwright
> *The Matchmaker*, Act II

Most of the change we think we see
in life
Is due to truths being in or out
of favor.

> Robert Frost (1874–1963)
> American poet
> "The Black Cottage"

24

RELIGION

All religions offer the key to the good life, but whether they bring the good life to their believers and supporters depends on how these people interpret the meaning of their religion. Sometimes they do things in the name of their religions which do not appear religious, or good. I cannot conceive of a truly religious act doing harm. I cannot fault the religion for harm done in its name, but only those who fail to understand the religious message. Those who honor their religion as a source of wholesome faith and of constructive performance toward all other people earn my deepest respect.

My theology, briefly, is that the universe was dictated, but not signed.

Christopher Morley (1890–1957)
American author and editor
Quoted in *More Funny People*
by Steve Allen, 1982

I'm an atheist, and I thank God for it.

George Bernard Shaw (1856–1950)
Irish playwright
Quoted in *The Book of Unusual Quotations* by Rudolf Flesch

Religion is what keeps the poor from murdering the rich.

Napoleon Bonaparte (1769–1821)
Emperor of France

Trust in Allah, but tie your camel.

Arab proverb

If a man has really strong faith, he can indulge in the luxury of skepticism.

Friedrich Nietzsche (1844–1900)
German philosopher
The Twilight of Idols, 1888

The hardest job that people have to do is to move religion from their throats to their muscles.

———————

When I do good, I feel good; when I do bad, I feel bad. That's my religion.

Abraham Lincoln (1809–1865)
16th president of the United States

I count religion but a childish toy,
And hold there is no sin
   but ignorance.

> Christopher Marlowe (1564–1593)
> British dramatist
> Prologue to *The Jew of Malta*

Every day, no matter what I'm doing, I say, "Lord, I'll do the best I can, and You do the rest."

> Loretta Young (b. 1913)
> American actress

It's going to be fun to watch and see how long the meek can keep the earth after they inherit it.

> Frank McKinney "Kin" Hubbard (1868–1930)
> American caricaturist and humorist
> Creator of Abe Martin

Many bring their clothes to church rather then themselves.

God gives every bird its food, but He does not throw it into the nest.

> J.G. Holland (1819–1881)
> American author and editor

Coming out of a meeting they had attended together, the archbishop offered the cardinal a ride in his carriage. "After all," said the Anglican archbishop, "we both are engaged in God's work."

"Yes," replied the cardinal, "you in your way, and I in His!"

I have been driven to my knees many times because there was no place else to go.

Abraham Lincoln (1809–1865)

Everyman has three friends—children, his money, and his good deeds. When the time comes for him to leave the world he calls upon his children, who reply, "Don't you know that no one can conquer death?"

Then he calls upon his money, saying, "Day and night I have worked for you, save me now."

The money replies, "Wealth cannot deliver you from death."

He next calls on his good deeds and they reply "Go in peace. By the time you arrive in the next world, we will be there before you to offer you help."

The Talmud

Say not, if people are good to us, we will do good to them; but resolve that if people do good to you, you will do good to them, and if they oppress you, oppress them not again.

Mohammed (570–632 A.D.)
Arabian prophet and founder
of Mohammedan religion

Hermann Adler, a British rabbi, was sitting beside Cardinal Herbert Vaughan at an official luncheon. "Now, Dr. Adler," said the cardinal mischievously, "when may I have the pleasure of helping you to some ham?"

"At Your Eminence's wedding," was the reply.

Samuel Taylor Coleridge was involved in a discussion about religion. The other person believed that children should not be given formal religious education of any kind. They would then be free to select their own religion when they were old enough to decide. Coleridge did not bother to debate the point, but invited the man to see his rather neglected garden.

"Do you call this a garden?" asked his visitor. "There are nothing but weeds here."

"Well, you see," said Coleridge, "I did not wish to infringe on the liberty of the garden in any way. I was just giving the garden a chance to express itself and choose its own production."

Samuel Taylor Coleridge (1772–1834)
British poet

W.C. Fields, a lifetime agnostic, was discovered reading a Bible on his deathbed. "I'm looking for a loophole," he explained.

W.C. Fields (1879–1946)
American actor

25
RETIREMENT

It seems that the prevailing attitude toward retirement is changing. In times past, the older person seemed to look forward to and enjoy the role of elder statesman, critic, sage, and being the venerated guest in the home of his children. That was his rewarding retirement. Today, the idea of retirement is far less attractive; most of us like what we're doing and want to keep doing it until we can't. And yet the prospect of eventual retirement is exciting, too: Many are discovering that retirement is the beginning of a new career, and find themselves doing what they really wanted to do—but could not for most of their lives.

If the body holds up, I ain't going to quit until I get run over by a truck or a producer.

Jack Lemmon (b. 1925)
American actor

Retirement takes all the fun out of Saturdays.

> Duke Gmahle
> Quoted in *Say It Again!* by Jack Rosenbaum

When men reach their sixties and retire, they go to pieces. Women go right on cooking.

> Gail Sheehy (b. 1937)
> American author

Retirement is the time when if you chance to meet people who you worked with they greet you as they never did when you worked along with them, and it's the time they forget you were ever there when they don't see you.

———————

Retirement is the time where there is plenty of it, or not enough.

———————

Age-based retirement arbitrarily severs productive persons from their livelihood, squanders their talents, scars their health, strains an already overburdened Social Security system, and drives many elderly people into poverty and despair. Ageism is as odious as racism and sexism.

> Claude Pepper (b. 1900)
> Chairman, House Committee on Aging

Asked why he stopped playing football and retired, Johnny Unitas replied, "I could have played two or three more years. All I needed was a leg transplant."

> John Unitas (b. 1933)
> Quarterback, Baltimore Colts

When David Ben-Gurion came out of retirement for the ninth time, he was asked by an American why he bothered to retire.

"It's like those 'going out of business' signs you see along Seventh Avenue—a chance to unload stock he doesn't want, hire a new staff, and make a different contract with the union."

David Ben-Gurion (1886–1973)
First prime minister of Israel

After being defeated in 1945, Winston Churchill was offered a dukedom by the king and the greatly coveted Order of the Garter. He remarked, "Why should I accept the Order of the Garter from His Majesty when the people have just given me the Order of the Boot?"

Winston Churchill (1874–1965)
British statesman and prime minister

A man could retire nicely in his old age if he could dispose of his experience for what it cost him.

I have no thought of retiring. I may leave public office soon, but I will continue working. There is too much to be done. The world and its inhabitants are far too interesting to think of leaving them.

Carlos P. Romulo (1901–1985)
Philippine diplomat, educator,
and former president

Calvin Coolidge had to fill out a form confirming his membership in the National Press Club soon after he left the White House. In the space after "Occupation" he wrote "Retired." Next came "Remarks," where he filled in "Glad of it."

> Calvin Coolidge (1872–1933)
> 30th president of the United States

A professor of English at Harvard used to call his favorite liquor store each Friday night and greeted the clerk with the same sentence: "Hello. This is Charles Townsend Copeland. Send down a fifth of my usual." On the Friday of his retirement he made his regular call, with a change: "Hello. This is Charles Townsend Copeland. Do you know what emeritus means?"

"No," replied the clerk.

"It means on the shelf. Send down two fifths of the usual."

> Charles Townsend Copeland (1860–1952)
> American educator

To retire is to begin to die.

> Pablo Casals (1876–1973)
> Spanish cellist

26
THE RETORT

There are few exercises in speech that I enjoy more than the appropriate retort. Some situations cry out for a retort, but often there is no one skilled in the art to handle it. I'm blessed by being married to a woman who is rarely lost for words when a retort is called for. Nothing is more refreshing than the slapping-down of an untenable situation or re-mark with the sharpness of a cutting retort. This adds spice to life!

Jack Benny was invited to visit the White House. A guard stopped him and asked what he had in the violin case he was carrying.

"A machine gun," said Benny solemnly.

With the same solemnity, the guard said, "Oh, okay, enter. I was afraid for a moment that it was your violin."

Jack Benny (1894–1974)
American comedian

Myron, I wouldn't take your word for good morning till I looked out and saw the sun.

Alice K. Dormann

Tallulah Bankhead didn't like a review of one of her performances. She wrote to the critic: "I am sitting in the smallest room of the house. Your review is before me. Soon it will be behind me."

Tallulah Bankhead (1903–1968)
American actress

At a ceremony where a bust of Winston Churchill was dedicated, a buxom southern lady came up to the prime minister and said, "I traveled over a hundred miles for the unveiling of your bust."

Mr. Churchill gallantly replied, "Madam, I assure you, in that regard I would gladly return the favor."

Winston Churchill (1874–1965)
British statesman and prime minister

The hostess was playing the piano for her guests after dinner. One of the guests said to another, "What do you think of her execution?"

The other replied, "I'm in favor of it."

———

Lady Astor: "If I were your wife, I would put poison in your coffee."

Winston Churchill: "If you were my wife, I would drink it."

———

[136]

When Gladstone was British prime minister, he asked Queen Victoria to sign a bill passed by the House of Commons. Resenting his insistence, she retorted, "Mr. Gladstone, you forget. I am the queen of England!"

Gladstone replied; "Your Majesty, you forget who I am. I am the people of England."

William E. Gladstone (1809–1898)
British prime minister

A snobbish lady at a fancy dinner told a fellow guest, Rabbi Stephen S. Wise, that she was a member of the Daughters of the American Revolution. "My ancestors witnessed the signing of the Declaration of Independence," she said.

Dr. Wise replied, "This is very well. My ancestors witnessed the signing of the Ten Commandments."

Stephen S. Wise (1874–1949)
American rabbi and founder,
Jewish Institute of Religion

When Queen Anne elevated John Churchill to become the first Duke of Marlborough, some of the established nobility scorned him because of his humble parentage. On one occasion, one of them mocked, "Tell me, whose descendent are you?"

He replied: "Sir, I am not a descendent; I am an ancestor."

John Churchill (1650–1722)
British military commander

Once when Charles Lamb was speaking he heard a hiss from the audience. It was a distinguished group and an unexpected shock. After pausing briefly, he said, "There are only three things that hiss—a goose, a snake, and a fool. Come forth and be identified."

Charles Lamb (1775–1834)
British author

A gossip was complaining about her neighbor to a visiting friend. Her neighbor was so dirty, it was a disgrace to the neighborhood. "Just look, those clothes she has on the line and sheets and pillowcases all have black streaks up and down them."

Her guest said, "It appears, my dear, that the clothes are clean; the streaks you see are on your own windows."

———

William Randolph Hearst liked to have star guests for weekends at San Simeon. Once he invited Will Rogers whom he enjoyed introducing to his guests. A few days later, Hearst received a bill from Rogers for several thousand dollars for professional services. He called and protested, saying, "I didn't engage you as an entertainer. I invited you as my guest."

Rogers answered, "When people invite me as a guest, they invite Mrs. Rogers, too. When they ask me to come alone, I go as a professional entertainer."

Will Rogers (1879–1935)
American humorist

A proud mother remarked that her baby looked exactly like Winston Churchill. Hearing her say this, Churchill replied, "Madam, all babies look like me."

Winston Churchill (1874–1965)

Trust in God; She will provide.

Emmeline Pankhurst (1858–1928)
British suffragist

When Harry Cohn demanded of a group of writers their ideas on how to increase audiences at the Columbia movie houses and "get people out of the streets," Herman J. Mankiewicz retorted, "Why don't you show your movies in the streets, Harry? That'll drive them into the theaters!"

Frank Mankiewicz (b. 1924)
Executive VP, Gray & Company,
son of Herman J. Mankiewicz

27
SCIENCE

There never seems to be an end to the new wonders being discovered or developed by science. But, in recent years, as we witness the efforts of science we also become familiar with two frightening things: Science is not as exact as we thought it was, and some of its solutions foster problems that may pose even greater challenges. There are moments when the world stops to catch its breath, when we think that science has given us more in the last few decades than in all the preceding centuries. We think about these advances and, we wonder, are we really better for them?

Science is a first-rate piece of furniture for man's upper chamber, if he has common sense on the ground floor.

Oliver Wendell Holmes (1809–1894)
American writer and physician
The Poet at the Breakfast Table, 1872

If politicians and scientists were lazier, how much happier we should all be.

Evelyn Waugh (1903–1966)
British novelist

Science is the great antidote to the poison of enthusiasm and superstition.

Adam Smith (1723–1790)
Scottish economist and philosopher
The Wealth of Nations

The marvels of modern technology include the development of a soda can which, when discarded, will last forever, and a $7,000 car which, when properly cared for, will rust out in two or three years.

Paul Harwitz
The Wall Street Journal

Science is really going at a rapid pace. Now it's only a hundred years behind the comic strips.

Joey Adams (b. 1911)
American comedian

Aerodynamically speaking, the design of a bumblebee is a disaster. Too much body weight. Too little wing span. Just can't fly.
But it does.

Science is an exchange
of ignorance for that
Which is another kind of ignorance.

> George Gordon, Lord Byron (1788–1824)
> British poet
> *Manfred*

Scientists are peeping toms at the keyhole of eternity.

> Arthur Koestler (1905–1983)
> British author
> *The Roots of Coincidence*

In 1931, Charlie Chaplin and Albert Einstein drove down a street together. Pedestrians waved and cheered. Chaplin explained all of this: "The people are applauding you because none of them understands you, and applauding me, because everybody understands me."

> Charles Chaplin (1889–1977)
> British-born American actor

Mrs. Einstein visited Mount Wilson Observatory in California and pointed to a complex piece of equipment and asked what it was used for. The guide said it was used to determine the shape of the universe. "Oh," she said, not impressed, "my husband uses the back of an old envelope to work that out."

William Gladstone, watching Michael Faraday at an experiment which showed no practical result, asked, "Of what use is such a discovery?"

Faraday replied, "Why, sir, you will soon be able to tax it."

Michael Faraday (1791–1867)
British physicist and chemist

The wife of physicist Robert Millikan was passing through the hall of their home when she overheard the maid on the telephone.

"Yes, this is where Dr. Millikan lives, but he's not the kind of doctor that does anybody any good."

Robert A. Millikan (1868–1953)
American physicist, Nobel Prize winner

After all, we could get on very happily if aviation, wireless, television, and the like advanced no further than at present.... The sum of human happiness would not necessarily be reduced if for ten years every physical and chemical laboratory were closed and the patient and resourceful energy displayed in them transferred to the lost art of getting on together and finding the formula for making both ends meet in the scale of human life. Much, of course, we should lose by this universal scientific holiday...but human happiness would not necessarily suffer.

Edward A. Burroughs (1882–1934)
Bishop of Ripon
Sermon, at a meeting of the British Association
for the Advancement of Science,
Leeds, September 4, 1927

28
SUCCESS

The best part of success is that, whether we know it or not, all of us have been successful at something, perhaps many times, during our lives. I think the most difficult part of success is knowing when it is really ours. To be successful is to achieve an objective, but to be a success is always to have yet another objective in mind after you've achieved the last one.

We must believe in luck. For how else can we explain the success of those we don't like?

Jean Cocteau (1891–1963)
French author

We will be happy if we get around to the idea that art is not an outside and extra thing; that it is the natural outcome of a state of being; that the state of being is the important thing; that a man can be a carpenter and be a great man.

Robert Henri (1865–1929)
American artist

I encourage boldness because the danger of our se-
niority and pension plans tempt a young man to settle
in a rut named security rather than find his own
rainbow.

> Conrad Hilton (1887–1979)
> American hotelier

Nothing succeeds like the appearance of success.

> Christopher Lasch (b. 1932)
> American historian
> *The Culture of Narcissism*, 1979

After he had finished a concert and had gone back-
stage, Fritz Kreisler heard someone say, "I'd give my
life to play as you do!" He turned and looked at the
lady and said, "Madam, I did."

> Fritz Kreisler (1875–1962)
> American violinist

A Congressman said to Horace Greeley, "I am a self-
made man."
    Greeley replied, "That, sir, relieves the Almighty of a
great responsibility."

> Horace Greeley (1811–1872)
> American journalist and politician

The worst bankrupt in the world is the man who has
lost enthusiasm. Let him lose everything but enthusiasm and he will come through again to success.

If you achieve success, you will get applause. Enjoy it—but never quite believe it.

> Robert Montgomery (1904–1981)
> American actor

Everybody loves success, but they hate successful people.

> John McEnroe (b. 1959)
> Tennis champion

The taller a bamboo grows, the lower it bends.

———————

Anybody can win unless there happens to be a second entry.

> George Ade (1866–1944)
> American playwright and humorist

Behold the turtle: He only makes progress when he sticks his neck out.

> James Bryant Conant (1893–1978)
> American educator and president,
> Harvard University

The trick is to make sure you don't die waiting for prosperity to come.

> Lee Iacocca (b. 1924)
> Chairman of the board and CEO,
> Chrysler Corporation

We can't all be heroes, because somebody has to sit on the curb and clap as they go by.

Will Rogers (1879–1935)
American humorist

I never have frustrations.
The reason is to wit:
If at first I don't succeed,
I quit!

The public's appetite for famous people is a mouth as big as a mountain.

Robert Motherwell (b. 1915)
American artist

I make progress by having people around who are smarter than I am—and listening to them. And I assume that everyone is smarter about something than I am.

Henry J. Kaiser (1882–1967)
American industrialist

It's not enough to go to the plate—you have to have hits.

Anyone seen on a bus after the age of thirty has been a failure in life.

Loelia, Duchess of Westminster

The door to the room of success swings on the hinges of opposition.

———————

Strong lives are motivated by dynamic purposes; lesser ones exist on wishes and inclinations. The most glowing successes are but reflections of an inner fire.

Kenneth Hildebrand (b. 1906)
American clergyman

A diamond is a piece of coal that stuck to the job.

Opportunity is missed by most people because it is dressed in overalls and looks like work.

Thomas Edison (1847–1931)
American inventor

A Washington lady explained how to be a successful hostess: When your guests arrive say, "At last!" And when they leave say, "So soon!"

———————

I consider my ability to arouse enthusiasm among people the greatest asset I possess.

———————

To be agreeable, all that is necessary is to take an interest in other persons and in other things, to recognize that other people as a rule are much like one's self, and thankfully to admit that diversity is a glorious feature of life.

Frank Swinnerton (b. 1884–1982)
British novelist and critic

A man can fail many times but he isn't a failure until he begins to blame somebody else.

Without the element of uncertainty, the bringing off of even the greatest business triumph would be a dull, routine, and eminently unsatisfying affair.

J. Paul Getty (1892–1976)
American oil executive

Pleasure disappoints, possibility never. And what wine is so sparkling, who so fragrant, what so intoxicating, as possibility.

Sören Kierkegaard (1813–1855)
Danish theologian

Aviation is proof that given the will, we have the capacity to achieve the impossible.

Eddie Rickenbacker (1890–1973)
American aviator

Defeat isn't bitter, if you don't swallow it.

An interviewer was doing a piece on the reasons given by prominent men for their success. He told Clarence Darrow that most of the men he interviewed said that their success was due to hard work. Darrow thought and replied, "I guess that applies to me, too. I was brought up on a farm. One very hot day I was distributing and packing down the hay which a stacker was constantly dropping on top of me. By noon I was completely exhausted. That afternoon, I left the farm, never to return. I haven't done a day's hard work ever since."

Clarence S. Darrow (1857–1938)
American attorney

J. Paul Getty sent the following to a magazine requesting a short article explaining his success: "Some people find oil. Others don't."

J. Paul Getty (1892–1976)

Walter Hagen, who won and spent more than a million dollars during his career, was asked the secret of his success. He said, "You're here for only a short visit, so don't hurry, don't worry, and be sure to smell the flowers along the way."

Walter C. Hagen (1892–1969)
Golf professional

Liberace's 1954 Madison Square Garden concert was vastly appreciated by his fans, but critics blasted him. He told the critics, and has been repeating it ever since, "What you said hurt me very much. I cried all the way to the bank."

Wladziu Valentino Liberace (1919–1987)
American pianist

I don't know the key to success, but the key to failure is to try to please everyone.

Bill Cosby (b. 1937)
American comedian

I was taking a photograph of my wife with Haile Selassie. She was smiling, but he was grim. My wife whispered, "Please smile for the camera."

Selassie replied, "I never smile. Being a king is serious business."

Henry O. Dormann

It's nice to be important, but it's more important to be nice.

Trini Lopez (b. 1937)
American singer, musician

29

TALK

Talk, at its best, is a rare joy. At its worst,
talk is a bore which does nothing but
madden. Words wellspoken are an art
form I admire and seek to collect from
all the fascinating people I meet. My
only unhappiness about words used
well is that too many of them are soon
forgotten. I hope that we who listen will
endeavor to preserve those words for
others to share.

After many speakers and many words, it was George
Bernard Shaw's turn as the last speaker. After the applause subsided, he remarked, "Ladies and gentlemen,
the subject may not be exhausted. But we are." And he
sat down.

George Bernard Shaw (1856–1950)
Irish playwright

A minute of thought is worth more than an hour of
talk.

Channing Cox, who succeeded Calvin Coolidge as governor of Massachusetts, visited the vice-president. Cox asked him how he could see his visitors every day and manage to leave his office at five, while Cox could rarely leave before nine P.M.

Coolidge replied, "You talk back."

Calvin Coolidge (1872–1933)
30th president of the United States

If I had kept my mouth shut, I wouldn't be here.

Sign under a mounted fish

I'm not capable of blathering pap. I'm not happy or comfortable engaging in mush statements. If I'm going to say something, it's going to be substantive and at least provocative. Hopefully, it will also have some humor. That's my style. It's me.

Edward Koch (b. 1924)
Mayor of New York City

Gossip is the art of saying nothing in a way that leaves nothing unsaid.

President William Howard Taft was requested to attend a banquet and make a speech. The person inviting him said, "Just a brief one, Mr. President, since we can imagine how busy you must be—perhaps five minutes."

The president declined. "Do you realize that to prepare even a five-minute speech would take several hours to plan, to draft, to rewrite, to pass through channels for clearance? I'm afraid that I just haven't got the time."

The host persisted. "Well, as far as that goes, we'd be delighted to have you speak for an hour."

President Taft replied, "Gentlemen, I am ready now!"

William Howard Taft (1857–1930)
27th president of the United States and
Chief Justice of the Supreme Court
(Versions of this story have been attributed to Lincoln, other presidents, and other busy leaders.)

Who gossips to you will gossip of you.

———————

A gossip talks about others, a bore talks about himself, and a brilliant conversationalist talks about you!

Redbook magazine

A man stopped in a small town on his journey through Vermont and decided to join a group of men sitting on the porch of the general store. They were quiet. After several tries at starting a conversation and not succeeding, he asked, "Is there a law against talking in this town?"

One of them replied, "There's no law against talking, but we have an understanding that one doesn't speak unless he is sure he can improve on the silence."

O Lord, please fill my mouth with worthwhile stuff, and nudge me when I've said enough.

I can go on forever. To me, one thought becomes five hundred sentences.

Alice K. Dormann

Speech is conveniently located midway between thought and action, where it often substitutes for both.

John Andrew Holmes (1812–1899)
U.S. lawyer, brother of Oliver Wendell Holmes

No speech can be entirely bad if it is short.

Eloquence: saying the proper thing and stopping.

François de la Rochefoucauld (1613–1680)
French moralist
Maxims

When you hear that someone has gossiped of you, kindly reply that he did not know the rest of your faults or he would not have mentioned only these.

———————

Better to remain silent and be thought a fool than to speak out and remove all doubt.

> Abraham Lincoln (1809–1865)
> 16th president of the United States

It's a great art to know how to sell wind.

———————

The heart of a fool is in his mouth, but the mouth of a wise man is in his heart.

> Benjamin Franklin (1706–1790)
> American statesman and author
> *Poor Richard's Almanac*

To listen well is as powerful a means of communication and influence as to talk well.

> John Marshall (1755–1835)
> Supreme Court chief justice

Blessed is he who, having nothing to say, refrains from giving wordy evidence of the fact.

———————

Be sure your brain is in gear before engaging your mouth.

———————

What a big gap there is between advice and help.

———————

Dignity is the capacity to hold back on the tongue what never should have been in the mind in the first place.

Only if we can restrain ourselves is conversation possible. Good talk rises upon much self-discipline.

John Erskine (1879–1951)
American educator and writer

A barber asked King Archelaus how he would like his hair cut. "In silence," replied the king.

Archelaus (413–399 B.C.)
King of Macedonia

Tallulah Bankhead was very talkative. A magician, Fred Keating, once told friends, "I've just spent an hour talking to Tallulah for a few minutes."

Tallulah Bankhead (1903–1968)
American actress

A rather silly and very talkative woman was boring the actor, Lucien Guitry, with her constant chatter. "You know, I simply talk the way I think," she said.

"Yes, but more often," he replied.

Lucien Guitry (1860–1925)
French actor

His enemies might have said before that he talked rather too much; but now he has occasional flashes of silence that make his conversation perfectly delightful.

> Sydney Smith (1771-1845)
> British clergyman and author
> Writing on Thomas Macaulay (1800–1859),
> Scottish author and statesman

Governor Claude A. Swanson of Virginia had made a long and rambling speech. Afterwards a woman came up to the speaker's table to shake his hand. "How did you like my speech?" he asked.

She answered, "I liked it fine. But it seems to me you missed several excellent opportunities."

Swanson was puzzled. "Several excellent opportunities to do what?"

"To quit," she replied.

> Claude A. Swanson (1862–1939)
> Governor of Virginia

When the main portion of the meal was finished, the presiding person whispered to the first speaker, "Shall we let the people enjoy themselves a little longer, or would you like to deliver your speech now?"

Talk low, talk slow, and don't say too much.

> John Wayne (1907–1979)
> American actor
> Advice on acting

I should not talk so much about myself if there were anybody else whom I knew as well.

Henry David Thoreau (1817–1862)
American writer and philosopher
Walden, or Life in the Woods, 1854

30

TELEVISION

While television sometimes proves that some pictures aren't really worth ten thousand words, it does bring into our homes the faces and words of people and their leaders, whom we otherwise would never know. As a result, what is happening all over the world seems to be happening to each of us. The task created by this phenomenon is to make us act collectively to change the disturbing things television allows us to see. Television is a wondrous window on the world; hopefully we won't pull the blinds.

Television has proved that people will look at anything rather than each other.

Ann Landers (b. 1918)
Advice columnist

Television is the third parent.

R. Buckminster Fuller (1895–1983)
American architect and author

Television is a medium of entertainment which permits millions of people to listen to the same joke at the same time, and yet remain lonesome.

> T.S. Eliot (1888–1965)
> American-born English poet

Two friends met after many years. One was married, the other single. The married man asked the other, "How have you managed to stay single all this time?"

"It's not difficult," replied the bachelor. "Every time I watch a commercial on television I learn about women—that they are anemic, have stringy and broken hair, large pores, wrinkles, rough hands, underarm odor, and are overweight."

———

Television is a medium because well done is rare.

> Fred Allen (1894–1956)
> American comedian and radio star

My success on television was because, as an only child, I got into the habit of going on long walks and talking to myself. Television is a form of soliloquy.

> Kenneth Clark (1903–1983)
> British art connoisseur and author
> "Civilization" on public television

People used to watch television. Now it is just on.

> Reuven Frank (b. 1920)
> President, NBC News

Television is the first truly democratic culture available to everyone and entirely governed by what people want; the most terrifying thing is what people want.

> Clive Barnes (b. 1927)
> British-born American drama critic

I have never seen a bad television program, because I refuse to. God gave me a mind, and a wrist that turns things off.

> Jack Paar (b. 1918)
> Talk show host
> *TV Guide*

Television is a device that permits people who haven't anything to do to watch people who can't do anything.

> Fred Allen (1894–1956)

Television is the opiate of the masses.

———

Darling, turn on the boob tube.

———

Turn off the light, open the window, turn on the TV, and go to sleep.

31
TIME

Time is both common and rare; we either have too much or too little. None of
us believe we use it as well as we should.
But like all the other ingredients in life,
some time is for flavor and some time is
just to give support to all the other ingredients we mix in. Time's importance
is measured from where we sit when we
do the measuring. Unfortunately, we
frequently think to measure it after it is
used rather than before. Then we realize that time is not a common luxury at
all—but a rare and valuable gem.

A stockbroker urged Claude Pepper to buy a stock
that would triple in value in a year. Pepper told him,
"At my age, I don't even buy green bananas."
Claude Pepper (b. 1900)
Chairman, House Committee on Aging

To hurry is useless. The thing to do is to set out in time.
Jean de la Fontaine (1621–1695)
French author and fabulist

Time cannot be expanded, accumulated, mortgaged, hastened, or retarded.

Does't thou love life? Then do not squander time, for that is the stuff life is made of.

Benjamin Franklin (1706–1790)
American statesman and author
Poor Richard's Almanac

Hell, by the time a man scratches his ass, clears his throat, and tells me how smart he is, we've already wasted fifteen minutes.

Lyndon B. Johnson (1908–1973)
36th president of the United States

If we work upon marble, it will perish; if on brass, time will efface it; if we rear temples, they will crumble into dust; but if we work upon immortal minds, and imbue them with principles, with the just fear of God and love of our fellow men, we will engrave on those tablets something that will brighten to all eternity.

Noah Webster (1758–1843)
American lexicographer

A bishop was to make his first sermon at the court of Queen Victoria. He asked Disraeli for advice. "How long do you think my first sermon should last, Mr. Prime Minister?"

Disraeli replied, "If you preach for forty minutes, Her Majesty will be satisfied; for thirty minutes, she will be delighted. If you preach for only fifteen minutes, Her Majesty will be enthusiastic!"

Benjamin Disraeli (1804–1881)
British prime minister

A time of quietude brings things into proportion and gives us strength. We all need to take time from the busyness of living, even if it be ten minutes to watch the sun go down or the city lights blossom against a canyoned sky.

———

We need time to dream, time to remember, and time to reach the infinite. Time to be.

Gladys Taber (1899–1980)
American author

We are condemned to kill time: Thus we die bit by bit.

Octavio Paz (b. 1914)
Mexican poet and diplomat
Cuento de los Jardines, 1968

Time cools, time clarifies; no mood can be maintained quite unaltered through the course of hours.

Thomas Mann (1875–1955)
German author
The Magic Mountain, 1924

The time which we have at our disposal every day is elastic; the passions that we feel expand it, those that we inspire contract it; and habit fills up what remains.

Marcel Proust (1871–1922)
French author
Within a Budding Grove

Time is the school in which we learn. Time is the fire in which we burn.

Delmore Schwartz (1913–1966)
American poet
"For Rhoda," 1938

Time is a great legalizer, even in the field of morals.

H.L. Mencken (1880–1956)
American critic and author
A Book of Prefaces, 1917

Time has no division to mark its passage; there is never a thunderstorm or a blare of trumpets to announce the beginning of a new month or year. Even when a new century begins, it is only we mortals who ring bells and fire off pistols.

Thomas Mann (1875–1955)
German author
The Magic Mountain, 1924

We haven't the time to take our time.

Eugene Ionesco (b. 1912)
French author
Le Roi Se Meurt (Exit the King), 1963

Time is dead as long as it is being clicked off by little wheels; only when the clock stops does time come to life.

> William Faulkner (1897–1962)
> American author
> *The Sound and The Fury*, 1929

Time rushes toward us with its hospital tray of infinitely varied narcotics, even while it is preparing us for its inevitably fatal operation.

> Tennessee Williams (1914–1983)
> American playwright
> Foreword to *The Rose Tattoo*, 1950

32
TRUTH

How important is truth in today's
world? Sometimes it seems that the end
objective is more important than telling
the true facts, whether by individuals or
governments. Lack of truthfulness is
sometimes labeled "public relations" or
"politics." If it is either of these, such
professions are indeed poorly and un-
justly used. The public is most respon-
sive to the truth, the big truth. Savvy
politicians have found that out and use
it with joy as a weapon to slug their
opponents.
And, as a weapon, few objects have an
impact greater than the truth.

I never gave anybody hell. I just told the truth and they
thought it was hell.

Harry Truman (1884–1972)
33rd president of the United States

Most writers regard the truth as their most valuable possession, and therefore are economical in its use.

> Mark Twain (1835–1910)
> American humorist

He who foretells the future lies, even if he tells the truth.

> Arab proverb

When Leo Durocher was manager of the Dodgers he was booed for pulling a pitcher out in the eighth inning of a close game. A reporter later asked him how he felt about the crowd's reaction. He replied, "Baseball is like church. Many attend. Few understand."

> Leo Durocher (b. 1906)
> American baseball manager

Truth is still more effective than money in America. But it takes persistence.

> Thomas M. Devine (b. 1927)
> American businessman
> Government accountability project,
> a non-profit study group

If an ordinary person is silent about the truth, it may be a tactical maneuver. If a writer is silent, he is lying.

> Jarolav Seifert (b. 1901)
> Czech poet, Nobel Prize winner

All Cretans are liars.

> Epimenides (7th c. B.C.)
> A Cretan

I do not know what I may appear to the world. But, to myself, I see, to have been only like a boy playing on the seashore, diverting myself in now and then finding a smoother pebble or a prettier shell than the ordinary, whilst the great ocean of truth lay all undiscovered before me.

Sir Isaac Newton (1642–1727)
British physicist and mathematician
Supposedly his last words

Non-violence and truth [Satya] are inseparable and presuppose one another. There is no god higher than truth.

Mohandas K. Gandhi (1869–1948)
Indian leader and statesman
True Patriotism—Some Sayings of Mahatma Gandhi, 1959

There are very few human beings who receive the truth, complete and staggering, by instant illumination. Most of them acquire it fragment by fragment, on a small scale, by successive developments, cellularly, like a laborious mosaic.

Anaïs Nin (1903–1977)
French-born American author and diarist
Diary, 1940

Truth exists; only falsehood has to be invented.

Georges Braque (1882–1963)
French artist
Pensées sur l'Art

TRUTH

The truth is found when men are free to pursue it.

Franklin Delano Roosevelt (1882–1945)
32nd president of the United States
Address, February 22, 1936, Temple University

Truth has no special time of its own. Its hour is now—always.

Albert Schweitzer (1875–1965)
French medical missionary, author,
Nobel Peace Prize winner
Out of My Life and Thought, 1949

We seek truth and will endure the consequences.

Charles Seymour (1865–1963)
President, Yale University, 1937–1950

When you have eliminated the impossible, whatever remains, however improbable, must be the truth.

Sir Arthur Conan Doyle (1859–1930)
British author and creator of Sherlock Holmes
The Sign of Four, 1890

Wit has truth in it; wisecracking is simply calisthenics with words.

Dorothy Parker (1893–1967)
American author and wit
Writers at Work

Artistic growth is, more than it is anything else, a refining of the sense of truthfulness. The stupid believe that to be truthful is easy; only the artist, the great artist, knows how difficult it is.

Willa Cather (1873–1947)
American author
The Song of the Lark, 1915

The passion for seeking the truth only for truth's sake ... can be kept alive only if we continue to seek the truth for truth's sake.

Franz Boas (1858–1942)
American anthropologist
Introduction to *Race and Democratic Society*, 1954

In human relations, kindness and lies are worth a thousand truths.

Graham Greene (b. 1904)
British author
The Heart of the Matter, 1948

33
WAR

There are those who can argue well that wars are necessary, that they even exist among animals and birds and insects as nature's way of keeping things in balance. Man's progress is hastened by war, argue others, because science is pushed into doing more. Perhaps.

But in my mind, the benefits of war are the camouflage war employs to justify its existence. The day war becomes old-fashioned and obsolete is the day man will become civilized.

You can no more win a war than you can win an earthquake.

Jeanette Rankin (1880–1973)
American suffragist and legislator

When two elephants fight, it is the grass underneath that suffers.

African proverb

You can't say civilization don't advance—in every war they kill you a new way.

Will Rogers (1879–1935)
American humorist
Autobiography

A horse, cow, and donkey argued about who had made the greatest contribution to the war effort. The horse said he made it possible for men to ride off to war, and the cow said she kept the civilian population alive. The donkey claimed the greatest recognition, for, he said, "If I had not been at the head of governments, there would not have been a war!"

———————

It is the boldness of the soldier that makes the general great.

Italian saying

Nothing except a battle lost can be half so melancholy as a battle won.

Arthur Wellesley, Duke of Wellington (1769–1852)
British military leader
Dispatch from the field, Waterloo, 1815

War is a series of catastrophies that results in a victory.

Georges "The Tiger" Clemenceau (1841–1929)
French statesman
Quoted in G. Suarez's *Clemenceau*, 1886

I'd like to see the government get out of war altogether and leave the whole field to private industry.

> Joseph Heller (b. 1923)
> American author
> *Catch 22*

War is a highly cooperative method and form of theft.

> Jacob Bronowski (1908–1974)
> Polish-born English philosopher

The time to win a fight is before it starts.

> Frederick W. Lewis

War is the continuation of politics by other means.

> Karl von Clausewitz (1780–1831)
> Prussian general

The object of war is not to die for your country but to make the other bastard die for his.

> George S. Patton (1885–1945)
> American general
> as quoted in the film *Patton*

When the French film actor, Jean Gabin, arrived in New York during World War II he was asked what the French thought of the British. He replied, "We are both pro-British and anti-British. Those who are pro-British say every night in their prayers, 'Dear God, let the gallant British win quickly,' and those who are anti-British pray 'Dear God, let the filthy British win very soon.' "

Jean Gabin (1904–1976)
French actor

Heathcote William Garrod, a professor at Oxford, was working at the Ministry of Munitions during World War I. At this time white feathers were handed to able-bodied men not in uniform. Garrod was given one by a woman with this comment: "I am surprised you are not fighting to defend civilization."

He replied, "Madam, I am the civilization they are fighting to defend."

Heathcote William Garrod (1878–1960)
British classical scholar

In October, 1944, the Japanese issued statements that most of the American Third Fleet had been sunk or was retiring. Admiral William F. Halsey issued the following counterstatement: "Our ships have been salvaged and are retiring at high speed towards the Japanese fleet."

William F. Halsey (1882–1959)
Pacific naval commander, World War II

The artist Frederic Remington, sent by William Randolph Hearst to cover the war in Cuba in 1898, found nothing happening when he arrived. He cabled asking Hearst if he should return.

Hearst cabled back: "Please remain. You furnish the pictures, and I'll furnish the war."

> William Randolph Hearst (1863–1951)
> American newspaper publisher

This war, like the next war, is a war to end war.

> David Lloyd George (1863–1945)
> British prime minister

Like German opera, too long and too loud.

> Evelyn Waugh (1903–1966)
> British author
> Reply when asked his impression of battle

War is not an instinct but an invention.

> José Ortega y Gasset (1883–1955)
> Spanish philosopher, writer, and statesman
> Epilogue, *The Revolt of the Masses*, 1930

War alone brings up to its highest tension all human energy and puts the stamp of nobility upon the peoples who have the courage to face it.

> Benito Mussolini (1893–1945)
> Italian dictator
> *Encyclopedia Italiana*, 1932

We must conquer war, or war will conquer us.

> Ely Culbertson (1891–1955)
> American bridge player
> *Must We Fight Russia*, 1946

Either man is obsolete or war is.

> Richard Buckminster Fuller (1895–1983)
> American architect and author
> *I Seem to Be a Verb*, 1970

Sometime they'll give a war and nobody will come.

> Carl Sandburg (1878–1967)
> American poet
> *The People, Yes*, 1936

In war there is no second prize for the runnerup.

> Omar N. Bradley (1893–1983)
> American general
> *Military Review*, September 1951

Older men declare war. But it is youth that must fight and die. And it is youth that must inherit the tribulation, the sorrow, and the triumphs that are the aftermath of war.

> Herbert Hoover (1874–1964)
> 31st president of the United States
> Speech at Republican National Convention,
>   Chicago, June 27, 1944

Training for combat is the single most important peacetime mission.

Charles H. Griffiths
Vice-admiral, U.S. Navy, deputy chief of Naval Operations (Submarine Warfare)

34
WEALTH

I've seen many enjoy a feeling of wealth
no matter how little money they have.
Wealth well used is a delight to observe;
wealth unused is sad to see. Wealth, to
me, is not in the having, but in the using.
The greatest joy is to see a man with
ideals and dreams making wonders happen by using his wealth not as an instru-
ment of vanity, but as a plaything of
pride and joy.

If you want to find out about bargains, ask a million-
aire. That's how he got that way.

Henry O. Dormann
People Do

Could I climb to the highest place in Athens, I would
lift my voice and proclaim, "Fellow citizens, why do
you turn and scrape every stone to gather wealth and
take so little care of your children to whom one day
you must relinquish it all."

Socrates (470–399 B.C.)
Greek philosopher

There must be more to life than having everything.

> Maurice Sendak (b. 1928)
> American children's book author and illustrator
> *Higglety, Pigglety, Pop, Or There Must Be
> More to Life*

Wealth is the fuel that keeps the new people moving faster than the speed of worry.

———————

Behind every fortune there is a crime.

> Honoré de Balzac (1799–1850)
> French author
> *Le Pere Goriot*, 1835

Bernard Baruch went to his father to tell him he had made his first million. His father did not seem impressed.

"I am not even thirty and I already have my first million—and you're not even happy?" Baruch asked.

His father replied, "No, my son, I am not impressed. What I want to know is how you will spend it."

> Bernard M. Baruch (1870–1965)
> American statesman and financier

A banker warned the British poet Robert Graves that one could not grow rich writing poetry. He replied that if there was no money in poetry, there was certainly no poetry in money, and so it was all even.

> Robert Graves (1895–1985)
> British poet and novelist

Wealth is not his that has it, but his that enjoys it.

> Benjamin Franklin (1706–1790)
> American statesman and author
> *Poor Richard's Almanac*

You can never be too thin or too rich.

> Mrs. William "Babe" Paley (1915–1978)
> Wife of William S. Paley, CBS Chairman

A man is rich according to what he is, not according to what he has.

———

In the long run, it is better to be born lucky than to be born clever or rich.

> W. Somerset Maugham (1874–1965)
> British author

Fortune does not change men. It only unmasks them.

———

A light purse is a heavy curse.

> Benjamin Franklin (1706–1790)
> *Poor Richard's Almanac*

Some men still have their first dollar. The man who is really rich is the one who still has his first friend.

———

The richer your friends, the more they will cost you.

> Elisabeth Marbury (1856–1933)
> American playwright
> *Careers for Women*

If you get up early, work late, and pay your taxes, you will get ahead—if you strike oil.

> J. Paul Getty (1892–1976)
> American oil executive

You can live well if you're rich and you can live well if you're poor, but if you're poor, it's much cheaper.

> Andrew Tobias (b. 1947)
> American author

Don't knock the rich. When did a poor person give you a job?

> Dr. Laurence J. Peter (b. 1919)
> American author and psychologist

The weak shall inherit the earth—but not the mineral rights.

> J. Paul Getty (1892–1976)

The more you get, the more you got to take care of.

> Alice K. Dormann

There are many in this old world of ours who hold that we all get the same amount of ice. The rich get it in summertime and the poor get it in winter.

> Anonymous

Do you spend more than you make on things you don't need to impress people you don't like?

He who multiplies riches multiplies care.

> Benjamin Franklin (1706–1790)
> *Poor Richard's Almanac*

Asked when a wealthy man has enough money to be happy, J.P. Morgan replied, "When he has made the next million."

> J.P. Morgan (1837–1913)
> American financier

He that waits upon fortune is never sure of dinner.

> Benjamin Franklin (1706–1790)
> *Poor Richard's Almanac*

A man who has a million dollars is as well off as if he were rich.

> John Jacob Astor (1763–1848)
> American financier

Speaking of railroad tycoon E.H. Harriman: "I have all the money I want and he hasn't."

> John Muir (1838–1914)
> American naturalist

One of the wealthiest men in the world, Nubar Sarkis Gulbenkian, was filling out a form from a research firm. In the space following "Position in life" he filled in "Enviable."

> Nubar Sarkis Gulbenkian (1896–1972)
> British industrialist and philanthropist,
> son of Calouste Gulbenkian, who
> financed the Gulbenkian Foundation
> for the arts, science, and education

Making money is easy; losing weight is hard.

35
WISDOM

Wisdom is a rare quality. Seeing wisdom at work in others is a delight, for true wisdom works to harm no one and help everyone. The only unhappy thing about wisdom is that so few of us bother to use it.

When I was a boy of fourteen, my father was so ignorant I could hardly stand to have the old man around. But when I got to twenty-one, I was astonished at how much he had learned in seven years.

Mark Twain (1835–1910)
American humorist

Every man is a damn fool for at least five minutes every day; wisdom consists in not exceeding the limit.

Elbert Hubbard (1856–1915)
American writer and publisher

A good scare is worth more to a man than good advice.

E.E. "Ed" Howe (1853–1937)
American editor and novelist

Wisdom is the reward you get for a lifetime of listening when you'd have preferred to talk.

Doug Larson
United Press International

Everybody is ignorant—but only on different subjects.

———

Wisdom consists in knowing what to do with what you know.

———

I had a monumental idea this morning, but I didn't like it.

Samuel Goldwyn (1882–1974)
American movie producer

The only fool bigger than the person who knows it all is the person who argues with him.

———

Experience is the name everyone gives to their mistakes.

Oscar Wilde (1854–1900)
Irish author and wit
Lady Windemere's Fan

There is a story in Arabic which tells of a pupil asking a wise man how he could become a good conversation-alist. The sage replied, "Listen, my son."

After waiting a while, the pupil said, "I am listening. Please continue your instruction."

The sage smiled. "There is no more to tell."

[187]

Wise men don't need advice. Fools won't take it.

Benjamin Franklin (1706–1790)
American statesman and author

God, give us grace to accept with serenity the things that cannot be changed, courage to change the things which should be changed, and the wisdom to distinguish one from the other.

Dr. Reinhold Niebuhr (1892–1971)
American pastor and theologian
The Serenity Prayer, 1943, in the monthly bulletin
  of the Federal Council of Churches, after a sermon,
  Congregational Church, Heath, Massachusetts

A gentleman saw a blind woman standing on a busy city corner waiting for someone to help her cross the intersection. He stepped up to her and asked, "May I go across with you?"

Two brothers went to a judge to settle their dispute on the division of the estate left to them by their father. The judge ruled: "Let one brother divide the estate, and let the other brother have first choice."

An optimist is a person who sees a green light everywhere. The pessimist sees only the red light. But the truly wise person is color blind.

Albert Schweitzer (1875–1965)
French medical missionary, author,
Nobel Peace Prize winner

If we were logical, the future would be bleak indeed. But we are more than logical. We are human beings, and we have faith, and we have hope, and we can work.

Jacques Cousteau (b. 1910)
French naval officer, explorer

36
WOMEN

Ah! Here is a topic that has as many experts as there are subjects. There are few men and fewer women who have not spoken somewhat authoritatively on the subject of women. Opposite men's declaration that you can't live with them and you can't live without them is the point of view claiming that without women, men would be empty shells—lifeless, dull, and nonproductive. Comments at these two extremes—and in between— are plentiful.

It seems obvious from the start that I should use my womanness as an asset rather than a liability.

Estée Lauder
Founder of the cosmetic firm

The best way for a husband to clinch an argument is to take her in his arms.

She's uglier than most computers.

Alice K. Dormann

Women will remain the weaker sex just as long as they're smarter.

_____

Some women work so hard to make good husbands that they never manage to make good wives.

_____

A woman worries about the future until she gets a husband, while a man never worries about the future until he gets a wife.

_____

Women's styles may change but their designs remain the same.

_____

When I prepare to go to sleep, everything comes off or out.

Phyllis Diller (b. 1917)
American comedian

We won't marry the boy with a camel
nor even the one with two donkeys.
We're going to marry the boy
who comes to take us away in a Mercedes.

African folk song

One good husband is worth two good wives; for the scarcer things are, the more they're valued.

> Benjamin Franklin (1706–1790)
> American statesman and author

A lady said that second thoughts are always best, and most people agreed with her. Then she explained. Man was God's first thought; woman was his second.

———————

It is said that a good woman inspires a man, a brilliant woman interests him, a beautiful woman fascinates him, but a sympathetic woman gets him.

———————

A woman's chastity consists, like an onion, of a series of coats.

> Nathaniel Hawthorne (1804–1864)
> American author

Chauncey Depew, after an eloquent speech, was surrounded by women. One of them said, "In your speech you said sleep was the most beautiful thing in the world. I thought you'd say a woman was."

Depew thought a moment, and then replied, "Next to a beautiful woman, sleep is!"

> Chauncey M. Depew (1834–1928)
> American lawyer, legislator, orator

In 1968, when the Jets won the championship of the American Football League, they had a party. Each married player, when he spoke, gave a glowing tribute to his wife for her understanding, patience, and help during the season.

Joe Namath, the team's famous bachelor, then spoke, "And, I want to thank all the good-looking broads in town."

Joe Namath (b. 1943)
former Quarterback, New York Jets

A member of the British Parliament welcomed Lady Astor as she took her seat there on her first day as the first woman ever to be elected. "Welcome to the most exclusive men's club in Europe!" he said.

"It won't be exclusive long." Lady Astor smiled. "When I came in, I left the door wide open!"

Nancy Witcher Langhorne Astor (1879–1964)
American-born member,
British House of Commons

You can never tell about a woman, and if you can, you shouldn't.

———————

The proper study of mankind is woman.

Henry Brooks Adams (1838–1918)
American historian

Whilst Adam slept
    Eve from his side arose
Strange his first sleep
    would be his last repose.

———————

The errors of women spring, almost always, from their faith in the good or their confidence in the true.

> Honoré de Balzac (1799–1850)
> French author

The happiest women, like the happiest nations, have no history.

> George Eliot (1819–1880)
> British author
> *The Mill on the Floss*, 1860

So many beautiful women and so little time.

> John Barrymore (1882–1942)
> American actor

Being a woman is a terribly difficult trade, since it consists principally of dealing with men.

> Joseph Conrad (1857–1924)
> British author

The great fault in women is the desire to be like men.

> Joseph Marie de Maistre (1753–1821)
> French author and politician

Women are strange and incomprehensible—invented by Providence to keep the wit of men well sharpened by constant employment.

> Arnold Bennett (1867–1931)
> British author and critic

If I were asked to what the singular prosperity of the American people is to be mainly attributed, I should reply: to the superiority of their women.

> Alexis de Tocqueville (1805–1859)
> French historian
> *Democracy in America*, 1835

Women are lookingglasses possessing the magic and delicious power of reflecting the figure of man at twice its natural size.

> Virginia Woolf (1882–1941)
> British author
> *A Room of One's Own*

A lady is one who never shows her underwear unintentionally.

> Lillian Day (b. 1893)
> American writer
> *Kiss and Tell*

If women didn't exist, all the money in the world would have no meaning.

> Aristotle Onassis (1900–1975)
> Greek shipping magnate

Women are a decorative sex; they never have anything to say, but they say it charmingly.

> Oscar Wilde (1854–1900)
> Irish author and wit
> *The Picture of Dorian Gray*

Thanks to feminism, woman can now acquire status in two ways: through marriage or their own achievements. Cure cancer or marry the man who does, either way society will applaud. Unless he marries into the British royal family, it doesn't work that way for men. Wives shed no glory on their husbands. Having tea with Nancy Reagan is an honor; having tea with Dennis Thatcher is a joke.

Katha Pollitt (b. 1949)
American writer

There are only three things to be done with a woman. You can love her, suffer for her, or turn her into literature.

Lawrence Durrell (b. 1912)
British author

Whatever women do they must do it twice as well as men. Luckily, this is not difficult.

Charlotte Whitton (1896–1975)
Canadian government official

Women are the only oppressed group in our society that lives in intimate association with their oppressors.

Evelyn Cunningham
Speech, New York, May 16, 1969

In Canton, when a typical young woman says she is looking for a man with three highs, she is thinking less of Chinese ideology than of a high salary, a high educational level, and a height of at least five feet, seven inches.

When man and woman die, as poets sung,
his heart's the last part moves,
her last, the tongue.

> Benjamin Franklin (1706–1790)
> *Poor Richard's Almanac*

A girl told her sweetheart that she would not marry him until he had saved a few thousand dollars. Several months later, she met him on the street and asked him how much he had saved.

He replied, "Thirty-five dollars."

Blushing, she said, "Well, I guess that's near enough."

I married beneath me. All women do.

> Nancy Witcher Langhorne Astor
> (1879–1964)

A lady tried to embroil Sir John Mahaffy in a feminist argument by saying to him, "You are a man. I am a woman. What is the essential difference between us?"

"Madam," he replied, "I can't conceive."

> Sir John Pentland Mahaffy (1839–1919)
> Irish scholar

There is no female mind. The brain is not an organ of sex. As well speak of a female liver.

> Charlotte Perkins Gilman (1860–1935)
> American author
> *Woman and Economics*, 1898

The female woman is one of the greatest institooshuns of which this land can boast.

Artemus Ward (Charles Farrar Browne) (1834–1867)
American humorist

The female of the species is more deadly than the male.

Rudyard Kipling (1865–1936)
British author
The Female of the Species, 1911

God created man, and finding him not sufficiently alone, gave him a female companion so that he might feel his solitude more acutely.

Paul Valèry (1871–1945)
French author
Tel Quel, 1943

The great question ... which I have not been able to answer, despite my thirty years of research into the feminine soul, is "What does a woman want?"

Sigmund Freud (1856–1939)
Austrian founder of psychoanalysis
Conversation with Marie Bonaparte

Who knows what women can be when they are finally free to become themselves? Who knows what women's intelligence will contribute when it can be nourished without denying love? The time is at hand when the voices of the feminine mystique can no longer drown out the inner voice that is driving women on to become complete.

> Betty Naomi Friedan (b. 1921)
> American writer and spokesperson on women
> *The Feminine Mystique*, 1963

Women and elephants never forget an injury.

> Hector Hugh Munro (Saki) (1870–1916)
> British author
> "Reginald in Russia," 1910

Faithful women are all alike; they think only of their fidelity, never of their husbands.

> Jean Giraudoux (1882–1944)
> French playwright and author
> *Amphitryon 38*, 1929

The fickleness of the women I love is only equaled by the infernal constancy of the women who love me.

> George Bernard Shaw (1856–1950)
> Irish playwright
> *The Philanderer*, 1893

Most women are not so young as they're painted.

> Max Beerbohm (1872–1956)
> British author and wit
> *A Defense of Cosmetics*

Women are wiser than men because they know less and understand more.

James Stephens (1882–1950)
Irish author
The Crock of Gold, 1930

Men are irrelevant. Women are happy or unhappy, fulfilled or unfulfilled, and it has nothing to do with men.

Fay Weldon
British author
Down Among the Women

37
WORDS

Artistry with words is more of a skill than artistry with paints. A painter can correct and refine and add subtle tones to what he uses his brush to say, but spoken words are final. As they leave the tongue, they are finished and cast forever, no matter what other words may follow. Written words, too, are not easily presented.

How often do we search in vain for a word to bring a thought properly to paper? Some writers settle for less; other writers live in pain because they feel they haven't found the magnificent words their minds won't surrender.

Admire words well used: They are living monuments to the power of the minds of men.

Man does not live by words alone, despite the fact that sometimes he has to eat them.

Adlai Stevenson (1900–1965)
American statesman

Here comes the orator with his flood of words and his drop of reason.

> Benjamin Franklin (1706–1790)
> American statesman and author

Words in haste do friendships waste.

_____

Man is master of the unspoken word, which spoken, is master of him.

_____

One day, while shaving, Mark Twain cut himself. He recited his entire vocabulary of swear words. His wife, hoping to stun him, repeated all the swear words. Then, Twain turned to her and said, "You have the words, my dear, but you don't know the tune."

> Mark Twain (1835–1910)
> American humorist

When, in 1906, Douglas MacArthur was the aide-de-camp to President Theodore Roosevelt, he asked him what he felt was the single factor that accounted for his popularity with the public.

Roosevelt replied, "To put into words what is in their hearts and minds, but not in their mouths."

> Theodore Roosevelt (1858–1919)
> 26th president of the United States

A reporter, coming upon a big story, telegraphed his editor. The editor replied, "Send six hundred words."

The reporter wired back, "Can't be told in less than twelve hundred words."

The editor replied, "Story of creation of world told in six hundred. Try it."

The best way to keep one's word is not to give it.

Napoleon Bonaparte, (1769–1821)
Emperor of France

A Chinese sage said that "if language is not used correctly, then what is said is not meant; if what is said is not meant, then what ought to be done remains undone; if this remains undone, morals and art will be corrupted; if morals and art are corrupted, justice will go astray and the people will stand about in helpless confusion."

Only a brilliant man knows whether the applause for his words is politeness or appreciation.

During World War II, the Civil Defense authorities had posters printed which read: "Illumination must be extinguished when premises are vacated." When he saw these signs, President Franklin Roosevelt exclaimed, "Damn, why can't they say 'Put out the lights when you leave'?"

Franklin Delano Roosevelt (1882–1945)
32nd president of the United States

Horace Greeley had a linguistic quirk, insisting that the word "news" is plural. He once sent a cable to a member of his *Tribune* staff: "Are there any news?"
    The reply came back: "Not a new."

> Horace Greeley (1811–1872)
> American journalist and politician

One of the favorite stories James Thurber told is of a conversation he had with a nurse while he was in a hospital. "What seven-letter word has three u's in it?" he asked.
    The nurse thought a while, and then replied, "I really don't know, but it must be unusual."

> James Thurber (1894–1961)
> American author and cartoonist

Originality is not seen in single words or even sentences. Originality is the sum total of a man's thinking or his writing.

> Isaac Bashevis Singer (b. 1904)
> Polish writer

A powerful agent is the right word. Whenever we come upon one of those intensely right words in a book or newspaper the resulting effect is physical as well as spiritual, and electrically prompt.

> Mark Twain (1835–1910)
> *An Essay on William Dean Howells*, 1906

To the man with an ear for verbal delicacies—the man who searches painfully for the perfect word, and puts the way of saying a thing above the thing said—there is in writing the constant joy of sudden discovery, of happy accident.

H.L. Mencken (1880–1956)
American critic and author

The word-coining genius, as if thought plunged into a sea of words and came up dripping.

Virginia Woolf (1882–1941)
British author
The Common Reader, 1925

Look out how you use proud words. When you let proud words go, it is not easy to call them back. They wear long boots, hard boots.

Carl Sandburg (1878–1967)
American poet
"Primer Session," 1922

I don't care how much a man talks, if he only says it in a few words.

Josh Billings (1818–1885)
American humorist
Josh Billings: His Sayings, 1865

Short words are best and old words when short are best of all.

Winston Churchill (1874–1965)
British statesman and prime minister

No one means all he says, and yet few say all they mean. For words are slippery and thought is vicious.

> Henry Brooks Adams (1838–1918)
> American historian
> *The Education of Henry Adams*, 1907

The English language is rather like a monster accordion, stretchable at the whim of the editor, compressible ad lib.

> Dr. Robert Burchfield, (b. 1923)
> Editor, *Oxford English Dictionary*,
> fourth and final supplement
> London, May 8, 1986

Communication. It is not only the essence of being human but also a vital property of life.

> John A Pierce
> Northern Telecom Corporation

38
WORK

Perhaps the most easily accepted differences among us are our criteria for the quality of work *we* perform and that which others perform in working *for* us or with us. We expect other people's standards to be different from ours and measure by how closely their standards come to ours. Work without quality is wasted. Children enjoy building sandcastles by the edge of the sea, but when the tide comes in and begins to destroy their work, they are overcome with tears and desperately try to improve the quality of their work with sandwalls built around their castle.

We, too, build sandcastles. And each one that we build teaches us what we must do to make the next one better.

Work is the greatest thing in the world. So we should save some of it for tomorrow.

Don Herold (b. 1927)
American museum director

The world is full of willing people. Some willing to work, the rest willing to let them.

> Robert Frost (1874–1963)
> American poet

A mule will labor ten years willingly and patiently for you, for the privilege of kicking you once.

> William Faulkner (1897–1962)
> American author

I am a great believer in luck and the harder I work the more I have of it.

> Stephen Leacock (1869–1944)
> Canadian humorist and economist

My father taught me to work; but he did not teach me to love it.

> Abraham Lincoln (1809–1865)
> 16th president of the United States

Work is more fun than fun.

> Noel Coward (1899–1973)
> British playwright and actor

What we're trying to do is nothing more than what we try to teach our children. Good manners; be polite, be pleasant, treat anybody the way you'd like to be treated yourself, is really what we must put across.

> Isadore Sharp (b. 1931)
> President and CEO, Four Seasons Hotels

What counts is not the number of hours you put in, but how much you put in the hours.

I like to work half a day. I don't care if it's the first twelve hours or the second twelve hours. I just put in my half every day. It keeps me out of trouble.

Kemmons Wilson (b. 1913)
CEO, Holiday Inns

Every man's work is a portrait of himself.

It's a recession when your neighbor loses his job; it's a depression when you lose your own.

Harry S. Truman (1884–1972)
33rd president of the United States

Work is the best narcotic.

The real essence of work is concentrated energy— people who really have that in a superior degree by nature are independent of the forms and habits and artifices by which less able and active people are kept up to their labors.

Walter Bagehot (1826–1877)
British economist and journalist

The brain is a wonderful organ; it starts the moment you get up in the morning and does not stop until you get to the office.

Robert Frost (1874–1963)

Some who are not paid what they are worth ought to be glad.

———————

The harder I work, the luckier I get.

Samuel Goldwyn (1882–1974)
American movie producer

An idea is not worth much until a man is found who has the energy and the ability to make it work.

———————

Whatever is worth doing at all, is worth doing well.

Philip Dormer Stanhope, fourth Earl of
Chesterfield (1694–1773)
British statesman
Letters to His Son, 1774

People who work sitting down get paid more than people who work standing up.

Ogden Nash (1902–1971)
American humorist

Labor, if it were not necessary for existence, would be indispensable for the happiness of man.

Samuel Johnson (1709–1784)
British journalist, poet, and critic

Too many people quit looking for work when they find a job.

———————

WORK

The French work to live, but the Swiss live to work.

A French woman

His genius he was quite content
In one brief sentence to define:
Of inspiration one percent,
Of perspiration, ninety-nine.

Thomas Edison (1847–1931)
American inventor
Golden Book, April 1931

If I miss one day's practice, I notice it. If I miss two days, the critics notice it. If I miss three days, the audience notices it.

Ignance Paderewski (1860–1941)
Polish pianist and statesman

If you have a job without aggravations, you don't have a job.

Malcolm Forbes (b. 1919)
American publisher and financier

One of the symptoms of an approaching nervous breakdown is the belief that one's work is terribly important.

Bertrand Russell (1872–1970)
British mathematician and author

The feeble tremble before opinion, the foolish defy it, the wise judge it, the skillful direct it.

Mme. Jeanne Roland de la Platière
(1754–1793)
French Girondist, 1791–1793

Hard work never killed anybody, but why take a chance?

Charlie McCarthy (Edgar Bergen)
(1903–1978)
American ventriloquist

As regards intellectual work, it remains a fact, indeed, that great decisions in the realms of thought and momentous discoveries and solutions of problems are only possible to an individual, working in solitude.

Sigmund Freud (1856–1939)
Austrian founder of psychoanalysis

When I was a young man, I met Franklin Roosevelt and Harry Truman. I remarked to Mr. Truman that I thought Mr. Roosevelt was a wonderful man.

Mr. Truman agreed. "Franklin likes me despite my shortcomings in my work, and I like him because he has none."

Henry O. Dormann

39
WRITING

Writing in some educated societies is an art as common as the art of breathing. However, few of us write as well as we breathe, but many of us think we do. What is the measure of great writing? Is it the ability to move people to activity? Or is it enough to capture the mind and relieve it, for a spell, of the problems of daily life? Or is it, like other art, something to admire and treasure because it is done well?

For me, writing is the mind put on paper so that it can be shared. It is as varied as the thoughts of man, and serves as many purposes as there are needs to be served.

Writing is a fuel for man. So, then, writing *is* like breathing: We need both to survive.

Writing is turning one's worst moments into money.
J.P. Donleavy (b. 1926)
Irish author

For $2.3 million, I'd be happy to say nasty things about everyone I know, too.

> Michael Kinsley
> Editor, *New Republic*
> Review of David Stockman's new book, *New York Times Book Review*, May 11, 1986

Manuscript: something submitted in haste and returned at leisure.

> Oliver Herford (1863–1935)
> American humorist and illustrator

If you wish to be a writer, write.

> Epictetus (55–135 A.D.)
> Greek philosopher

Unprovided with original learning, unformed in the habits of thinking, unskilled in the arts of composition, I resolved to write a book.

> Edward Gibbon (1737–1794)
> British historian

The art of writing is the art of applying the seat of the pants to the seat of the chair.

> Mary Heaton Vorse (1881–1966)
> American author

In composing, as a general rule, run your pen through every other word you have written; you have no idea what vigor it will give to your style.

> Sydney Smith (1771–1845)
> British clergyman and author
> *Lady Holland's Memoir*, 1855

[214]

I love being a writer. What I can't stand is the paperwork.

Peter De Vries (b. 1910)
American author

I am a camera with the shutter open, quite passive, recording, not thinking.

Christopher Isherwood (1904–1985)
British author
The Berlin Stories, 1939

If I tried to live by writing, I'd have been a head of whitened bones long ago.

Philip Larkin (b. 1922)
British poet

There is *no* way that writers can be tamed and rendered civilized. Or even cured. In a household with more than one person, of which one is a writer, the only solution known to science is to provide the patient with an isolation room, where food can be poked at him with a stick. Because, if you disturb the patient at such times, he may break into tears or become violent. Or he may not hear you at all...and if you shake him at this stage he bites.

Robert A. Heinlein (b. 1907)
American author

The reason why so few good books are written is that so few people who can write know anything.

Walter Bagehot (1826–1877)
British economist and journalist
Literary Studies

I do most of my writing sitting down. That's where I shine.

Robert Benchley (1889–1945)
American humorist

A writer who is afraid of mind, which English-speaking writers tend to be, unlike their Continental counter-parts, is a lion afraid of meat.

Paul West (b. 1930)
British educator

Writers have two main problems. One is writer's block, when words won't come at all, and the other's logor-rhea, when the words come so fast that they hardly get to the wastebasket in time.

Cecilia Bartholomew
San Francisco writer and teacher

I write to understand as much as to be understood. Literature is an act of conscience. It is up to us to re-build with memories, with ruins, and with moments of grace.

Elie Wiesel (b. 1928)
Romanian-born author and
spokesman on the Holocaust

If a person is not talented enough to be a novelist, not smart enough to be a lawyer, and his hands are too shaky to perform operations, he becomes a journalist.

Norman Mailer (b. 1923)
American author

Asking a working writer what he thinks about critics is like asking a lamppost how it feels about dogs.

> Christopher Hampton (b. 1946)
> British playwright
> London *Sunday Times*, October 16, 1977

I have made this letter longer because I lack the time to make it shorter.

> Blaise Pascal (1632–1662)
> French philosopher and mathematician
> *Lettres Provençals*, (1656–1657)

A person who publishes a book appears willfully in public with his pants down.

> Edna St. Vincent Millay (1892–1950)
> American poet

The creative urge is the demon that will not accept anything second-rate.

> Agnes de Mille (b. 1908)
> American choreographer and dancer

The trouble with our young writers is that they are all in their sixties.

> W. Somerset Maugham (1874–1965)
> British author
> *The Observer*, October 14, 1951

I never read a book before reviewing it. It prejudices one so.

> Sydney Smith (1771–1845)
> British clergyman and author

I found your essay to be good and original. However, the part that was original was not good and the part that was good was not original.

Samuel Johnson (1709–1784)
British journalist, poet, and critic

There are two kinds of books: those that no one reads and those that no one ought to read.

H.L. Mencken (1880–1956)
American critic and author

INDEX

INDEX

INDEX

Hayes, Helen, 6
Hazlitt, William, 43
Hearst, William Randolph, 82,
    116, 177
Heilman, E. Bruce, 68
Heine, Heinrich, 35
Heinlein, Robert A., 215
Heller, Joseph, 175
Hellman, Lillian, 91, 101
Helmsley, Leona, 20
Henderson, Verne E., 25
Henri, Robert, 144
Herford, Oliver, 214
Herold, Don, 207
Hershfield, Harry, 6
Hildebrand, Kenneth, 148
Hilton, Conrad, 70, 145
Hitler, Adolph, 45
Holland, J. G., 128
Holmes, John Andrew, 155
Holmes, Oliver Wendell, 140
Holmes, Oliver Wendell, Jr., 61,
    62, 66
Hoover, Herbert, 12, 29, 178
Hope, Bob, 5
Howe, E. E. "Ed," 81, 186
Howells, William Dean, 100
Hubbard, Elbert, 81, 196
Hubbard, Frank "Kin," 83, 128
Huxley, Aldous, 56
Huxley, T. H., 88

I

Iacocca, Lee, 23, 146
Imperatore, Arthur E., 26
Ionesco, Eugene, 166
Isherwood, Christopher, 215

J

James, William, 123, 124
Jaques, Elliot, 21
Jefferson, Thomas, 113, 114

Jensen, John, 123
Johnson, Lyndon B., 164
Johnson, Samuel, 26, 38, 50,
    210, 218
Jones, Thomas, 49

K

Kaiser, Henry J., 147
Kanin, Garson, 5
Kempton, Sally, 76
Kennedy, Edward M., 10
Kennedy, John F., 17, 23, 103,
    105, 106
Khashoggi, Adnan M., 23
Khomeni, Ayatollah, 37
Kierkegaard, Sören, 149
Kim, Ki-Jung, 24
King, Martin Luther, Jr., 5, 46,
    59, 70
Kinsley, Michael, 214
Kipling, Rudyard, 61, 198
Kirkpatrick, Jeane, 107
Kirkpatrick, Robert D., 56
Kissinger, Henry, 105
Koch, Edward, 104, 153
Koestler, Arthur, 142
Kreisler, Fritz, 145

L

Lamb, Charles, 138
Lancaster, Burt, 40
Landers, Ann, 112, 160
Lao-tzu, 66, 67
Larkin, Philip, 215
Larson, Doug, 187
Lasch, Christopher, 145
Lauder, Estée, 37, 190
Leacock, Stephen, 208
Lemmon, Jack, 131
Lewis, Frederick W., 175
Liberace, 150
Lincoln, Abraham, 10, 67, 127,
    129, 156, 208

INDEX

INDEX

INDEX

ABOUT THE COMPILER

There is possibly no one on Earth who personally knows as many of the world's leaders in government, business, labor, art, and education, as Henry O. Dormann. Much of his work as president and editor-in-chief of *Leaders* magazine involves traveling around the world to meet and talk with these extraordinary people.

He has come to know many world leaders well, sharing confidences, ideas, and good conversation. They have told him some of their innermost feelings and concerns, and they have shared *bon mots*—many of which appear in this book.

Mr. Dormann is an unusual man interested in the unusual and the great things of the world. Not a cynic, he is proud of the human race and its accomplishments. He is a positive man, feeling that if societies can laugh at their faults and concentrate on positive achievements, the world, gradually, will become a happier place. This collection reflects that rich and positive attitude.

Mr. Dormann is a man of unique talents and achievements. He was founder and the first executive director of the Library of Presidential Papers. He has served as president of the United States Technical Developments Company, a division of U.S. Banknote Corporation; chairman of the board of the *National Enquirer*, largest circulated newspaper in the United States; president and editor-in-chief of Sipa News Services; president and editor-in-chief of *Holiday* Magazine; chairman of the Haitian Development Corporation; chairman of Sabador, Inc., Liberia; chairman of the New York Assembly Council on Economic Development; Chairman of the International Board of Industrial Advisors; and president and editor-in-chief of *Leaders* magazine.